Becoming an Outstanding English Teacher

Becoming an Outstanding English Teacher supports all English teachers in offering a wide range of approaches to teaching and learning that will stimulate and engage students in studying English.

It offers practical strategies that can be used instantly in English lessons. The topics offer examples for questioning, differentiation and assessing progress. Some of the ideas have also been incorporated into lesson plans using texts from the revised English National Curriculum.

With a strong focus on creativity and engagement, this book covers:

- promoting thinking and independent learning skills in students
- methods to check learning rather than doing in the classroom
- techniques for personalising learning for students
- creating an environment for behaviour for learning.

Fully up to date with the National Curriculum guidelines and packed with practical strategies and activities that are easily accessible, this book will be an essential resource for all English teachers who are aiming to deliver outstanding teaching and learning continuously in their classrooms.

Kate Sida-Nicholls was an English teacher for eighteen years and had various roles in English departments. She has been the programme leader of a teacher training course for the past four years in Suffolk and Norfolk and spends a significant amount of time in classrooms with qualified and trainee teachers.

Becoming an Outstanding Teacher
Series Editor: Jayne Bartlett

Becoming an Outstanding English Teacher
Kate Sida-Nicholls

Becoming an Outstanding Mathematics Teacher
Jayne Bartlett

Becoming an Outstanding English Teacher

Kate Sida-Nicholls

Routledge
Taylor & Francis Group

LONDON AND NEW YORK

First published 2017
by Routledge
2 Park Square, Milton Park, Abingdon, Oxon OX14 4RN

and by Routledge
711 Third Avenue, New York, NY 10017

Routledge is an imprint of the Taylor & Francis Group, an informa business

British Library Cataloguing in Publication Data
A catalogue record for this book is available from the British Library

Library of Congress Cataloging in Publication Data
Names: Sida-Nicholls, Kate, author.
Title: Becoming an outstanding English teacher / Kate Sida-Nicholls.
Description: New York, NY : Routledge, 2016.
Identifiers: LCCN 2016007798| ISBN 9781138916968 (hardback) | ISBN 9781138916975 (pbk.) | ISBN 9781315689319 (ebook)
Subjects: LCSH: English language--Study and teaching--Great Britain. | English language--Study and teaching--Curricula--Great Britain. | English teachers--In-service training--Great Britain. | Curriculum planning--Great Britain. | Classroom environment--Great Britain.
Classification: LCC LB1576 .S4146 2016 | DDC 428.0071--dc23
LC record available at https://lccn.loc.gov/2016007798

ISBN: 978-1-138-91696-8 (hbk)
ISBN: 978-1-138-91697-5 (pbk)
ISBN: 978-1-315-68931-9 (ebk)

Typeset in Melior
by GreenGate Publishing Services, Tonbridge, Kent

Contents

List of figures and tables   ix

Acknowledgements   xi

Introduction   xii

1   Making connections   1

What makes a lesson outstanding?   2

The learning journey   4

What's in it for me?   6

References   7

2   How does it all begin?   8

Bell work   8

Learning outcomes   12

Starter activities   14

Big Question   15

Checking prior knowledge of students at the start of the lesson   15

Starter activities   18

Review   21

Contents

Summary: start of the lesson   22

Reference   22

3   Learning in the main   23

Sequencing the learning   24

The main assessment activity   26

Summary   36

References   36

4   So how does it all end?   37

Learning outcomes   37

Brilliant outcome   38

Big Question   39

Plenary activities   40

Reflection   43

Home learning   45

Summary   48

5   What's in a question?   49

Learning outcomes as questions   49

Teacher acting as a funnel for question and answer sessions   51

'Pose, Pause, Pounce, Bounce' question strategy   52

Depth of Knowledge   54

Written questions in poetry or other texts   56

Answering questions   58

Students generating their own questions   58

Summary   60

References   61

6   How do I know?   62

What is assessment?   63

Learning outcomes and success criteria   64

Quality of interactions with students   69

Encouraging reflection time   70

Marking as a form of assessment   72

Assessment without levels   73

Summary   75

References   75

7   Thirty different minds in the classroom   76

Differentiation by questioning   78

Differentiation by task   80

Differentiation by learning outcomes   82

Challenge/extension task   84

Differentiation with students with specific learning needs   84

Support notes   86

Visual images   86

Working with teaching assistants   86

Summary   88

Reference   88

Contents

8 The classroom environment   89

Classroom displays   89

Student contribution in lessons   90

Group work   91

Seating plans   93

Positive learning environment   93

Classroom assistants   94

Outside learning   96

Summary   98

Reference   99

9 Putting it all together   100

Key Stage 4 lesson plan   101

Key Stage 3 lesson plan   106

Summary   111

Reference   111

Conclusion   112

Index   113

Figures and tables

Figures

2.1   Jigsaws as a bell work activity   10

2.2   Pictures as a bell work activity   10

2.3   Bell work – dingbats   11

2.4   My level of understanding continuum line   14

2.5   My level of understanding is …   17

3.1   Summary of learning in the main   36

5.1   'Quickdraw' from *Rapture* by Carol Ann Duffy   57

7.1   List of assessable verbs from Ginnis   80

8.1   Setting behaviour expectations   98

Tables

2.1   KWL Grid   18

3.1   RAFT Grid   27

3.2   Six Thinking Hats   28

3.3   Make a poem from a Source of Words   34

3.4   Tic-Tac-Toe activities   35

4.1   Progress chart   41

Figures and tables

5.1   Depth of Knowledge levels   55

5.2   Depth of Knowledge levels in *Lord of the Flies*   55

6.1   An Entrance Ticket for the start of a Year 7 lesson on nouns   68

6.2   An Exit Ticket for the end of a Year 7 lesson on nouns   68

7.1   Working with learning support assistants in English lessons   87

8.1   Creating a positive classroom environment   94

8.2   Working with additional adults   95

9.1   Lesson plan using 'Quickdraw' by Carol Ann Duffy   101

9.2   Teaching persuasive techniques   106

Acknowledgements

My thanks to my English friends, Andrea, Kerensa, Maéve, Sarah-Louise and Trevor, who all took their part in contributing to this book.

I would like to thank Henry and Michael for giving me the time to write this book as it took longer than we all thought.

I would also like to thank my English colleagues and trainees, past, present and future as I know what you do every day in your English lessons makes a difference.

Introduction

During my career, I have had the privilege of working with a range of teachers, including those who are qualified and those who are still training. Being part of many teachers' classrooms has confirmed to me that teachers want to do the best they can for their students and work incredibly hard in order to do this on a daily basis.

Therefore, I have written this book as a way of helping to contribute to the range of resources that could make your life slightly easier in the classroom. Teaching day after day without much input from colleagues or engaging with purposeful and relevant continuous professional development can become draining. It can make you feel that you are teaching the same kind of thing and using the same sort of activities day after day. This book will hopefully engage your interest and stimulate you to try something slightly different in your classroom.

This book has the title 'Becoming an outstanding teacher' but that doesn't mean that you need to read this book in order to become one. If you are looking for ways of doing things slightly differently in your teaching then you are likely to already be an outstanding teacher or well on the way to becoming one. An outstanding teacher is a reflective teacher. So, if you are constantly looking for ways of improving your practice and seeking feedback from students and colleagues about the impact of your teaching then you definitely have the characteristics of an outstanding teacher. Therefore, the aim of this book is to help you build on your existing practice by providing you with some strategies that you might not have thought of before.

Chapter 1 discusses some of the key ideas in education at the moment and defines what outstanding teaching and learning might look like over time. Chapter 2 provides strategies for ascertaining the students' knowledge at the start of a lesson. It provides ideas for creating the right behaviour for learning at the start of the lesson and how important sharing the 'brilliant outcome' (not just the outcomes) with students can be for all students. Chapter 3 is full of practical strategies for teaching the main part of a lesson and covers a range of ideas that you can just pick up and include in a lesson plan. Chapter 4 identifies how important it is to demonstrate progress by ascertaining what the students have learned rather than what they have done by the end of the lesson. Chapter 5 outlines ideas for incorporating questioning strategies into teaching and even provides scenarios of what questioning can look like in a classroom when done well. It also includes subject specific questions to use when teaching Carol Ann Duffy's poem 'Quickdraw'. Chapter 6 focuses on assessment and the importance of success criteria if meaningful peer and self assessment is going to take place in a lesson. Chapter 7 is about differentiation and how knowledge of your students is essential to personalising the teaching and learning for students. Chapter 8 discusses the importance of the classroom environment and some strategies for establishing the right behaviour for learning are outlined. Finally, Chapter 9 contains lesson plans that incorporate the strategies that have been outlined in the book. Again, 'Quickdraw' by Carol Ann Duffy forms one lesson plan and there is another one about persuasive language aimed at KS3. I have written them as two lesson plans but realise that they may take longer than one lesson depending on your context.

I was an English teacher for eighteen years with various roles in schools and English departments and have now been running a teacher training programme for four years working with trainee and also qualified teachers in various contexts. The ideas and strategies in this book are practical and I know that they work in a range of classrooms as I, and others, have had the opportunity to use them in our teaching on a regular basis. I hope you feel after reading this book that it contributes to your classroom teaching in either a big or small way and helps you to become an outstanding teacher.

CHAPTER 1

Making connections

The job of an English teacher is one of the more high profile and accountable teaching roles in any school. Changes in the educational world are inevitable but what remains static is that English is always going to be the most important subject, along with Mathematics. On one level, it is because schools' results and reputations rely on the outcomes of the two subjects but more importantly, being literate to a good level and all that entails is the key to success in anyone's life.

Communication, whether reading, writing or speaking, is an essential skill that any young person needs to have in order to be successful in the ever changing twenty-first-century world. Employers state that young people need to be able to work collaboratively; make decisions based on evidence; assimilate a range of information in a short space of time; manage their time; present a clear point of view etc. The list goes on but all of these skills can be explicitly taught within the subject of English.

However, the unique feature of teaching English is that not only do we teach skills but we also teach about knowledge. We are able to give our students a rationale to their current world. We can give teenagers an insight into the cultural and social lives that existed in previous centuries. We do this in the hope that it will allow our students to understand the factors that underpin their current world but equally to understand that many of the issues they are grappling with have challenged others for centuries before them. By making these links from the past to the present we can show them how literature is still relevant to their world today. We can help them understand that by developing a love of reading they are engaging with a personal experience and an insight into a range of worlds that are much more compelling than any antics that might take place on *Big Brother*.

We can demonstrate to our students how language has changed and explain the reasons why they speak the words despite the incomprehensible spelling patterns. We can show teenagers that although they use text speak and emoticons as a tool to create their own language identity, it is not something new. Social groups have been creating their own language as a tool to exclude others for centuries. Teaching English is an opportunity to open minds to ideas and issues that can prick and sometimes penetrate the often self-centred world of the average teenager.

As English teachers, we repeatedly use the phrase 'there is no wrong answer' and our teaching needs to provide students with the tools and knowledge to enable them to create a case for whatever answer they decide is the right one.

What makes a lesson outstanding?

There is no easy answer to this question any more as the Ofsted advice is not to grade lessons individually and there is an increasing opinion within the profession that no one lesson should be assessed by itself.

Outstanding teaching is about ensuring students make progress in their thinking, learning, attitudes and outcomes over time. Students' learning has to be developed by establishing what they already know; use appropriate strategies of scaffolding so that they can gain and retain the new knowledge. The Russian psychologist Lev Vygotsky called this approach, the Zone of Proximal Development (www.simplypsychology.org/Zone-of-Proximal-Development.html). There should be a consistency to outstanding teaching and learning as a student's Zone of Proximal Development should be extended on a continuous basis.

The progression of all students through their own individual Zone of Proximal Development may happen in one lesson but equally it might happen over a period of time. A variety of formative and summative strategies to assess the speed and depth of the learning can be used to ascertain the progress of students. However, what makes one lesson outstanding can be seen as a subjective judgment by an observer. Outstanding teaching and learning should be assessed over a period of time (could be one lesson or longer) but using information gained from a range of sources that might include learning outcomes, marking in books, exam results, students and other forms of quantitative data, e.g. photos of students' work.

This book identifies a number of strategies that can help develop teaching and learning to become outstanding in the sense that all students make significant progress in gaining new knowledge or skills within a certain lesson or a specified period of time. Schools may have their own individual criteria for assessing outstanding teaching and Ofsted has a framework for assessing the quality of teaching and learning in a whole school.

So what might outstanding learning look like in an English classroom?

Students will be able to:

- create their own individual response about a topic or text supported by appropriate evidence
- make comparisons between ideas either verbally or in writing
- demonstrate a confidence with language and use it to create certain effects
- be imaginative and creative with ideas and language
- embrace challenge and be prepared to make mistakes
- recognise progress and be able to take the 'next' steps
- work independently and think for themselves.

What might outstanding teaching look like in an English classroom?

Teachers will:

- be passionate and enthusiastic about the subject of English and the relevance and importance of it
- demonstrate a high level of subject knowledge and be able to extend and challenge students in their thinking
- scaffold learning so all students make progress from an established starting point
- address misconceptions
- have high expectations of all students
- make links to the outside world and other subjects
- use a wide range of resources and methods to engage students
- ask a number of questions to probe depth of learning
- use a variety of formative assessment methods to gain feedback about the level of learning from all learners at any one point
- adapt teaching quickly to respond to the students' feedback about their level of understanding
- encourage independence in students' learning
- develop a culture of behaviour for learning.

The learning journey

It is now a common cliché to mention the 'journey' as it appears to be a concept that the media values and discusses in many contexts.

However, as teachers we have always been aware of the journey that we and our students are on within a school. We also know that any learning journey is not on a straight trajectory from start to finish. Learning takes place in a cyclical fashion. Ideas and concepts need to be revisited on a continuous basis in order to achieve retention and a depth of understanding.

At the time of writing, assessment without levels is the biggest issue facing education. Identifying and then documenting the learning journey of students has become even more essential at this time. English departments now have the opportunity to redefine the content but also the expectations of learning due to the new National Curriculum and GCSE exams.

Defining the start and end point of the learning journey for specific groups of students within your school will be essential to ensuring success. A chance to provide a breadth of opportunities and relevance to material taught to students especially at Key Stage 3 has been given to English departments. Research suggests that teaching skills and knowledge through integrated schemes of work will be more successful than teaching specific units of work on grammar or poetry. A document called 'The Science of Learning' summarises current research on cognitive science about how students learn. This document suggests that 'interleaving' ideas and concepts into learning is a more effective method (www.deansforimpact.org/pdfs/The_Science_of_Learning.pdf; Deans for Impact (2015). *The Science of Learning*. Austin, TX: Deans for Impact).

At KS3 this could mean creating a scheme of work with the topic Fantasy that incorporates reading of literature, prose and poetry. Learning is demonstrated in the creation of various writing styles, e.g. sonnets, diary entries, newspaper articles, descriptive writing. Teaching of grammatical features such as superlative adjectives and compound sentences is initiated from the texts studied within the Fantasy unit. This would be in contrast to studying a unit of work that has the one focus of sonnets or descriptive writing.

A scheme of work provides the content of a learning journey for a student but the successful outcome of the journey can be defined by the ideas now known as developing a growth mindset with students. It is the concept originally introduced by the psychologist Dr Carol Dweck about defining the differences in attainment and behaviour between people who believe that hard work and effort can change attainment and those who believe that their intelligence is fixed. In an English context, it would be those students who always say that they are bad at spelling so use that as an excuse to hand in work with lots of misspelt words in it. They don't believe that memorising formation and shapes of words will help them to improve their spelling so they fall into the mindset that they will always underachieve as their spelling will never be good enough.

Carol Dweck has based her theory of growth mindsets on significant research. Adopting some of Dweck's findings and applying a growth mindset would help the students overcome their negative mindset about their spelling by providing praise about their effort to improve their knowledge of how words are constructed rather than only providing praise when they did better than expected in a spelling test. Carol Dweck's book *Mindset: How You Can Fulfill Your Potential* (2012) explains her theory and research about why employing a growth mindset approach in your classroom can help a student adopt a positive approach to their learning journey.

A learning journey is not just one that is restricted to students. What about your own learning journey? Observing other colleagues (not necessarily in your subject area) is essential to developing and improving your own practice once you have qualified. Teaching can be very a lonely job as very few other adults enter your classroom and give you feedback about the teaching and learning that is taking place in your classroom.

However, if you are able to observe another colleague then approach the observation with questions to help you improve your practice. Some suggestions could be:

- How is progress ascertained during the lesson?
- How are questions directed to students and which ones?
- How is the accountability of students in group activities established?
- How has a culture of equality between achievement and failure been developed?
- How is the behaviour of learning established?
- How do students give feedback about their quality and pace of learning?
- How does the teacher convey their passion and knowledge about their subject?
- How does the teacher convey to the students the relevance of what they are learning?

Another strategy is to observe the students in either an English teacher's lesson or a group of students from your class but in another subject. Try and ignore how the teacher is teaching and just focus on three or four students and observe how they make progress during a lesson.

Some kinds of questions to think about when doing this type of observation are:

- What kind of dialogue takes place between the students? How much time do they spend engaging in learning? How much off-task talk is there?
- Do the students engage positively with the activities?
- Do they learn anything new from the activities? How do you know?
- Do they demonstrate a positive or negative growth mindset in their approach to learning?
- Are there activities that clearly motivate students more or less?

Observing students in this way will enable you to see the impact that teachers' behaviours have on their students. Teachers can fall into the trap of thinking that just because words have come out of their mouths or they have asked students to complete an activity then learning has taken place. Observations of students will allow you to ascertain how learning is taking place and why it is happening which will help you to improve the quality of learning in your own lessons.

What's in it for me?

There is no doubt that teenagers appear to be more motivated when they understand the reasons for their learning. The excuse of 'it might come up in your Literature exam' is likely to wear thin after the students are faced with learning about poems in eight consecutive lessons. As discussed earlier in this chapter, the study of English and its many components allow us to make links to the world that the students live in. Being able to make topical links to events and issues is key to bringing English alive for many students. Being able to link ideas in Shakespeare plays to soap operas; discussing the behaviour of a celebrity with a similar theme in a novel or making links to rap music and poetry is just one of the many skills that English teachers need to have 'up their sleeves'.

Sharing ideas or dilemmas from your own writing or reading can also be a tool to engage students with the need for learning a specific skill or gaining knowledge. Teachers who share their reading or writing interests are all helping to share their passion and love of the subject, which helps the students to understand the impact of their learning outside the classroom.

Sharing stories of famous people and their struggles can also help students to develop the right growth mindset as discussed earlier in this chapter. Discuss the skills that the famous person now exhibits and summarise how they might have acquired those skills. Creating scenarios or giving a context for a task can also help with motivation. For example, asking students to write the script for a presentation for a new business idea. Could they relate it to ones that they might have seen on *The Apprentice*?

Never underestimate the impact of a prop in a lesson. Something as simple as a hat or a balloon can help the students to buy into the imaginative content of a lesson. For example, a small vase which can be used as bottle of poison to put at the end of a Conscience Alley activity about whether Juliet should take the poison or not can be very effective.

In the following chapters we will look at strategies that you might wish to try and then transfer into your teaching repertoire if you find them to be effective in developing a classroom culture where outstanding teaching and learning can take place.

References

Deans for Impact (2015) *The Science of Learning*. Austin, TX: Deans for Impact. www.deansforimpact.org/pdfs/The_Science_of_Learning.pdf
Dweck, C.S. (2012) *Mindset: How You Can Fulfill Your Potential*, London: Robinson.

CHAPTER 2

How does it all begin?

The very start of the lesson is key to setting the tone of the learning atmosphere in a lesson. Too often it is easy to get caught up in the moment of departure of one class and not focus on the entry of another one. It is this essential five minutes that can make all the difference to the behaviour of a class and setting the atmosphere for learning.

As teachers, we are told to start lessons that engage and stimulate the students. However, this can be difficult at times due to the staggered arrival time of students as we have to deal with 'admin' and behaviour issues.

Greeting students at the door as they enter with the bell work task on the board can allow for a calm entry to the class and gives you time to deal with issues of missing homework, lack of pens and latecomers etc. It means that the students are completing a learning activity that challenges them in a different way than perhaps a starter would.

A bell work task does not need to be always related to the topic of the lesson which is why it differs from the 'starter' of a traditional three part lesson. It can develop the skills of students by making them think in a different way but it need not be an 'introduction' to the topic of the lesson. I would suggest that it can be a 'stand alone' activity for the students so that they can engage in independent and creative thinking which is not necessarily subject related.

In this chapter, we will look at some successful bell work tasks to use at the very beginning of a lesson and then move on to starter activities that have an English focus.

Bell work

A bell work activity is a short activity that can be put on a whiteboard that will engage the students as soon as they enter the classroom. The activity must have easy to follow instructions that can be put on the board so there is no need for repetition of instructions from you. However, it should only last for about three to four minutes. This gives you enough time to 'meet and greet' at the door and deal with any issues while the rest of the class starts to engage with learning and it can help to set the right behaviour for the learning tone for the rest of the lesson.

A commonly used resource is a 'thunk'. 'Thunks' are simple looking questions about everyday things that are intended to make us look at things in a different light and they originated from the award winning author Ian Gilbert of *Independent Thinking* (www.independentthinking.co.uk). Ian Gilbert has published a book called *The Little Book of Thunks: 260 Questions to Make Your Brain Go Ouch* (2007). A couple of examples are – 'Is a blacked out window still a window?' Or another one – 'If I borrow a million pounds, am I a millionaire?' These questions can be put on the board with the instructions for the students to write their ideas down on their mini-whiteboards or on a piece of paper. However, I have found that it can take a few lessons using thunks as a bell work activity for the students to get used to the idea of thinking of answers to a question that does not immediately have a clear answer. The students will probably only need about three to four minutes thinking independently or in pairs before they will want to discuss the questions and share their ideas.

Linking visual images is another bell work task that students can complete with minimal input from you. For example, three images about WW1 can generate the following questions/ideas that you can ask the students to think/write about. Resources to use could be the picture *Gassed* by John Singer Sargent and words taken from 'Dulce Decorum Est' and put into a Wordle document www.wordle.net. For example, this activity could be used prior to a unit about WW1 poetry but equally it could work as a bell work task as it can be done any time as it is encouraging students to think, link and relate their current knowledge about WW1 literature.

- Are they able to make the connection that the pictures demonstrate WW1 in different ways?
- Can the students link them together in such a way that demonstrates their understanding of the propaganda surrounding WW1?
- Are they also able to make links between the *Gassed* painting by John Singer Sargent and a Wordle document about Wilfred Owen?
- What do they know about the use of gas in WW1? What do they know about the poets of WW1? What do they know about Wilfred Owen?

Another bell work activity that can be related to the lesson but doesn't require explanation from you is 'guess the learning objective' with pictures. The template for this jigsaw can be found on www.presentationmagazine.com and it is easy to put a picture underneath the jigsaw and then animate each puzzle piece so that the picture is gradually revealed (Figure 2.1).

How does it all begin?

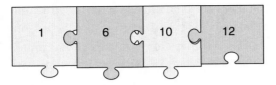

Figure 2.1 Jigsaws as a bell work activity

This sort of activity can create interest and curiosity from the students at the very beginning of the lesson which all help to create the right behaviour for learning atmosphere.

Another bell activity is to break down the learning objective into individual pictures that are set up as clues so that the students have to put it together to understand what the learning objective might be (Figure 2.2). This activity encourages the students to develop their linguistic knowledge to make links between the grammatical structure of words and images.

To continue setting up this activity, split up the words of the learning objectives into syllables and find appropriate images to put with them. Figure 2.2 spells out in syllables says 'Today we will'. The images can be put onto a PowerPoint slide without the clues underneath and then the students can spend about three to four minutes figuring it out. You can make it as easy or difficult as you wish.

Figure 2.2 Pictures as a bell work activity

Dingbats are another way of developing students' linguistic skills but they work well as a bell work activity as again they require little input from you. You can easily find them in newspapers but there are also some on www.tes.com.

Again, this is developing students' linguistic knowledge by asking them to make links between images and their understanding of words. It is also helping them to develop their understanding of idioms and their use in the English language. For example, the answer to the dingbat in Figure 2.3 is 'Standing in line'.

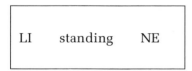

Figure 2.3 Bell work – dingbats

An Entrance Ticket can also be used for a bell work activity too. Each student is given a piece of paper 5 × 5 inches which has clear instructions about the bell work activity. The Entrance Ticket could include any of the following:

- a cloze procedure where students have to fill in the gaps using their knowledge about a certain topic or skill;
- an image or an extract of a text that needs to be annotated;
- a short poem in the style of a sonnet, using rhyming couplets, iambic pentameter;
- a Wordle full of key words for that lesson that need to be organised into a list.

However, if you are going to use an Entrance Ticket for a bell activity then the answers should not be reviewed once you stop the bell work task. It should be a stand alone activity which is helping the students to develop a culture of behaviour for learning and developing their English skills in various ways. If you want to check prior learning by using an Entrance Ticket then it is probably best used as part of a starter activity.

The aim of a bell work task is that it is something that the students can be doing with minimal input from you but equally takes up little time. Bell work is a successful method for reinforcing linguistic terms; key words or quotes that need to be learnt for GCSE exams. There is no need to review bell work at the start of the lesson. It should be viewed simply as a tool to develop the right culture for behaviour for learning and enhance learning rather than presenting new information. Reviewing bell work for any length of time can reduce the pace of the lesson and will defeat the purpose of having an engaging activity to help create the right atmosphere for learning.

Learning outcomes

Sharing learning outcomes with students is an important part of any lesson as everyone can see what is meant to be achieved by the end of the lesson. It also helps with ascertaining the progress in any lesson, if the learning outcomes that have been shared at the start of the lesson are then revisited at the end.

Learning outcomes are not learning objectives. A learning objective is essentially the topic of the lesson: 'Today we are going to learn about the character of Elizabeth Bennett in *Pride and Prejudice.*' The learning objective outlines the main learning topic of the lesson.

A learning outcome is about the development of the students' learning and how this has improved during the course of the lesson. The learning outcome should be focused on the 'learning' that is taking place in a lesson and not the 'doing' of the lesson. It should be measurable in some way so that the evidence is clear to assess and the progress of the students' learning noted.

A successful way of thinking about learning outcomes is to look at Bloom's Taxonomy which uses verbs such as evaluate, compare, solve, construct, classify and develop to help structure the progression of the learning. Using verbs in this way also makes it easier to differentiate the learning outcomes. It was created in 1948 by the psychologist Benjamin Bloom to help classify educational goals for students. However, in the 1990s Bloom's Taxonomy was revised again to illustrate the stages of learning by using active verbs. Both versions are commonly used http://epltt.coe.uga.edu/index.php?title=Bloom's_Taxonomy Paul Ginnis, in his *Teacher's Toolkit* (2002), provides a clear and thorough explanation and guidance of Bloom's Taxonomy. His document 'Learning Principles & Planning Prompts' (http://s290088243.websitehome.co.uk/ginnis/images/stories/ginnis/downloads/Learning%20Principles%20&%20Prompts.pdf) gives an overview of what to think about when planning. Page 6 of the document outlines a range of verbs that are measurable that can be used to create differentiated learning outcomes.

There are many ways to introduce learning outcomes and it is important that students take ownership of their outcomes and that assessment of learning tools is used to assess the students' progress against these learning outcomes. More specific examples are given in Chapter 7, Thirty different minds in the classroom.

For example, if studying *Pride and Prejudice* by Jane Austen, three types of learning outcomes could be presented to the students (using Paul Ginnis' document):

1)   Your learning outcome is to **locate** five key quotes in this extract about Elizabeth Bennett. **Define** why these five key quotes are important. Think about the way Elizabeth looks, talks and acts with other characters.

2) Your learning outcome is to **analyse** your choice of five key quotes and explain how they have an impact on you as the reader. What do we as a reader feel about Elizabeth Bennett? Do we like her or not? Why do we feel like this? Think about what she says and how she interacts with other characters.

3) Your learning outcome is to **compare** the five key quotes and **evaluate** how they achieve their effects on the reader. Which one is the most effective and why?

The words in bold indicate the verbs from Paul Ginnis' document and also illustrates how the learning outcomes have become more difficult. The outcomes are asking the students to essentially do the same work but in a slightly more complex way. The outcomes provide a challenge in a structured way. For example, if a student chooses the first outcome and completes it quickly, it is possible and appropriate to ask the student to complete the next outcome as they are being asked to add comments about how the quotes have an impact on the reader.

By presenting outcomes in this way, students are being asked to choose their own learning outcome and write it down, but how do you monitor that and their progress against them?

Some strategies might be:

- Assign a specific colour Post-it note to each outcome and students choose the Post-it note that matches the colour of their chosen outcome. They then write down their learning outcome. The Post-it note is stuck to their desk and this quickly allows you to intervene if you think that the students have chosen an outcome that is too easy for them or perhaps too challenging? Try to avoid asking the students to write down their learning outcome on the Post-it note at this stage.

- The students could simply copy down their chosen learning outcome (rather than the learning objective) into the exercise book which can then be referred to throughout the lesson.

- Assign pictures or characters to certain learning outcomes. This tends to work with the younger years as they like referring to the characters or visual images when discussing the outcomes. Examples of this are given in Chapter 7, Thirty different minds in the classroom.

However, the brilliant learning outcome should be shared with students at this point of the lesson too. What does it look like when an extract has been written that compares and evaluates quotes? The brilliant learning outcome can be overlooked at the start of the lesson but it shouldn't be, as students need to know what they are hoping to achieve. Modelling can help with sharing the brilliant outcome and we look at this in Chapter 4, So how does it all end?

However, it is worth mentioning at this point too, as sharing the brilliant learning outcome is not always about modelling.

You might decide that sharing the criteria for A grade writing at GCSE is appropriate to demonstrate a brilliant outcome. Sharing the brilliant learning outcome means that all students are challenged when it is shared. As a colleague of mine says, 'sharing the brilliant learning outcomes means we don't "put lids on kids".' All students can be shown the brilliant learning outcome and if the learning outcomes are written as above, it means that all of the learning is accessible to a range of students in the classroom.

Another way of introducing the brilliant learning outcome is by outlining the skills you are expecting rather than the knowledge (Figure 2.4). The brilliant outcome is shown at one end and the students can mark themselves along the continuum at the start of the lesson and then again at the end of the lesson. However, when working with continuum lines, it does mean that questions should be asked of the students in order to rationalise their decisions about their placement on the continuum line. We will look in more detail at the use of continuum lines later in this chapter.

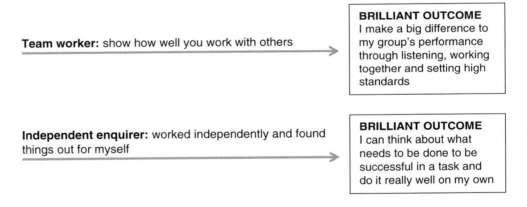

Figure 2.4 My level of understanding continuum line

Starter activities

A starter activity is the first point of assessment in a lesson and it should take no longer than seven to ten minutes of the lesson. It can act as a review of previous learning or be an activity that is set up to introduce new learning.

However, every starter section of a lesson should check the existing learning of the students. Different students retain varying amounts of information. In English, we are lucky to see our students more than once a week but equally that doesn't mean that the students have retained the information we think that they should have from one lesson to another. Starter activities should have a clear focus on establishing existing learning and exposing the gaps in the knowledge of the students. Central to outstanding teaching and learning in English is to find out the gaps in the knowledge of the students in the class in front of us and teach the missing information, instead of what we think a Year 9 class should know about a specific topic, e.g. Shakespeare.

Big Question

This is a key question that underpins your lesson. Linking back to the learning outcomes about *Pride and Prejudice*, a key question could be: 'Do we as a reader like Elizabeth Bennett? Why or why not?'

This question will be answered by the students by completing the learning outcomes as they will have to use evidence to justify their answer. Asking the students to put their answers in an envelope with their name on at the start of the lesson is a ready made plenary. You can pull out various answers from the envelope at the end of the lesson and ask students whether their views have changed from the start of the lesson. Students can justify their views by referring to the learning that they have gained during the course of the lesson.

There is no need to discuss the Big Question at the start of the lesson. The whole point of this activity is to gauge the existing knowledge from the students' answers to the Big Question. Another strategy to see what the whole class thinks is to use mini-whiteboards. Students can write down their answer to the Big Question on the mini-whiteboards at the start of the lesson. A clever strategy at this point of the lesson is to photograph the students holding up their mini-whiteboards so when you ask them the same question at the end of the lesson and they show you their whiteboards again, you can see who has changed their mind and ask them to justify it.

Checking prior knowledge of students at the start of the lesson

Presenting a quiz at the start of the lesson is an effective way of assessing the learning of the students and the term 'quiz' has more positive connotations than a test. A quiz that contains five or six questions, increasing in difficulty, is a very effective way of assessing prior knowledge. The key to this activity is to include a couple of questions that you think the students shouldn't know. The quiz should be constructed of brief questions. Equally, the answers should be short so that they can be viewed on a mini-whiteboard or heard succinctly from any student that you ask. If you are not going to use mini-whiteboards to ascertain answers but ask individuals then include some thinking time for all students after posing the first question and possibly a brief 20 second 'think and pair'. This will then allow you to ask any student without using hands-up, as taking answers from students with their hands up will only allow you to assess the knowledge of those students rather than of specific students in the class.

Some typical quiz questions might be:

1) What does 'onomatopoeia' mean?

2) 'The wind is a torrent of darkness' – is this a simile or a metaphor?

3) *Pride and Prejudice* is set in the Georgian, Victorian or Regency era?

4) Fill in the gaps of this quote: 'It is a truth _____, that a single man in possession of a good fortune, must be in want of _____.'

5) How is Mr Darcy described by other characters at the start of *Pride and Prejudice*?

6) Write down the three next events that happen in the novel after Lydia's elopement is discovered.

A quiz that is structured in this way will help you ascertain what knowledge is held by the students in the room. The questions are structured around knowledge (on various topics) rather than skills, as that is easier to assess and for the students to write down short answers.

Asking the students to answer questions that they don't have an answer to is perfectly acceptable at this early stage of the lesson. Asking the same questions at the end of the lesson, ensuring that you use strategies to assess all the learners in the classroom will be one way to demonstrate progress. It is tempting to only assess the students who have their hands up or are volunteering the answers. However, the key is to use Assessment for Learning (AfL) strategies that ensure that you are able to assess all of the learners, e.g. by the use of mini-whiteboards; no hands up; fingers held up to represent numbers (if options are given as answers, e.g. hold up three fingers if there are three options). The other strategy for ascertaining that you are assessing the knowledge of all the students is to ensure that you ask the students to indicate their answers on the mini-whiteboards or by holding fingers at the same time. Count down '1, 2, 3 and show me' – this means that all the class will indicate their learning to you at the same time rather than some students being able to copy others.

Another use of a quiz will be to help with the preparation of the closed book exam for the students too. A regular quiz of the key quotes of a set text will also help a greater percentage of the students demonstrate their recall of the quotes over a period of time. A weekly quiz on key quotes that you then repeat regularly will help to ensure that the quotations enter the students' long-term memory. This will avoid having to revise them closer to the exam when the quotations will only be in the students' short-term memory which could cause them to forget them in the stressful situation of an exam.

Another method to check the existing knowledge of students is to ask them to rate themselves against continuum lines (Figure 2.5). Ask the students to place themselves against both continuum lines at the start of the lesson.

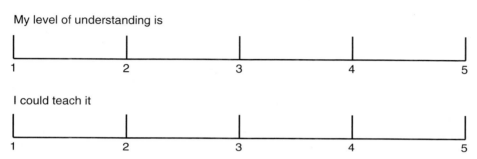

Figure 2.5 My level of understanding is …
(Source: John Hattie Visible Learning Conference November 2013)

However, before moving on from the continuum line a percentage of students need to be asked questions such as:

* Why have you made the decision to place yourself at that point on the continuum line at the start of the lesson?
* Where would you like to be on the continuum line?
* What do you need to do in order to achieve that target?
* You may wish to include what a 5 is – linking back to the brilliant learning outcome. What is a 5 on the continuum line in your context?

These types of questions to a number of students, perhaps the ones that represent specific groups in your class, will make them individually accountable for the decisions that they have made.

At a progress check point in the lesson (within about 15 minutes) ask either the same or different students the following questions:

* How far have you moved along the continuum line during the lesson?
* Do you know what you have done that has made you move along the line?
* What have I (teacher) done that has helped you move along the continuum line?
* Where would you like to be on the continuum line?
* What do you need to do in order to achieve that target?

You can then repeat some of these questions at the end of the lesson and especially focus on asking the students to reflect on what they have done in order to help them move along the continuum line.

Another strategy for checking prior learning is to use the KWL Grid. Design a table with headings as in Table 2.1. These activities ensure that checking students' prior knowledge is ascertained during the starter activity. Teachers can then teach to where the 'gap' is in the students' knowledge of the class in front of them rather than the expectations of a specific year group.

Table 2.1 KWL Grid

What I already **K**now	What I **W**ould like to know	What I have **L**earned
Students write in here in bullet points what they already know about a topic.	Having introduced the lesson to the students and asked them to choose their learning outcome, then ask them to complete this column.	At the plenary/review stage of the lesson, students fill in this section.

You can then discuss the points at the end of the lesson with the students, or they can stick this KWL Grid into their exercise book, or you can collect them in to check the existing learning and help to plan for future lessons.

Starter activities

The following activities can also be used at the start of the lesson but they do not necessarily have a focus on checking prior knowledge. These are strategies for introducing new knowledge that can be reinforced during the course of a lesson.

1) Buzz Word Bingo where students are asked to play 'bingo'. The aim of the game is to find the three key buzz words that you call out among other words that fill up the cards. The students should let you know when they have achieved three in a row. This link will help you generate bingo words with minimal effort. http://osric.com/bingo-card-generator/ This activity can be used as a starter activity as it can aid recall from previous learning or introduce new vocabulary or ideas that will be used in the forthcoming lesson. For example, grammatical or poetic terms.

2) Silent Debate is another successful starter activity. Before the students enter the room put out six pieces of sugar paper – each with a different question related to the learning objective or outcomes of the lesson. For example, if studying *Romeo and Juliet* as one of the set Shakespeare texts, you could ask the following open-ended questions:

- How far do you agree that Friar Lawrence was responsible for Romeo and Juliet's deaths?
- Do you think that Juliet should have just married Paris and forgotten about Romeo? What might have happened if she had?
- Do you think the nurse should have done more to protect Juliet?
- Do you think that if Romeo had received the message in Mantua he would not have killed himself?
- Do you think that Romeo should have accepted Tybalt's offer to a duel?
- Do you think the Capulet and Montague families should have done more to prevent the tragedy of Rome and Juliet's deaths? What could they have done?

Divide the students into small groups and give each group different colour pens or give each student a different colour pen. Then ask each group to work their way round each table writing down their views and responding to any previous points. However, they have to do it in silence. It is a Silent Debate. Students only spend two or three minutes at each table in order to create a healthy tension within the activity. The different colours from each group will allow you to see which group was the most engaged and confident in their opinions. If you have given each student a different colour pen then you will be able to ascertain the contribution of individuals and their confidence level by just looking at the individual sheets.

A variation on Silent Debate is to put a piece of paper on six tables with a different key question on each table, e.g. 'How far do you think that Friar Lawrence is responsible for the death of Romeo and Juliet?' Give the students whiteboard markers and then allow them to write on the tables around the piece of paper and write their response. Do this activity for about two or three minutes. The students then return to their original group and work out which idea is the best one that has been written on the table. They then feed this back to you as the teacher and you take photographs of the comments made on each table. Usually baby wipes will remove the pen off most tables and also windows if you wish to use windows.

The next step is to teach the rest of the lesson where you introduce various viewpoints about Friar Lawrence and encourage the class to think about their views. Then towards the end of the lesson, ask the same questions again from the Silent Debate activity and ask the students to annotate their answers in a similar way. You then take photos of these comments and upload them to your computer to compare with earlier answers. This will then form part of a very successful plenary that can demonstrate learning, as the evidence is obvious through the photographs. By asking the students to do a silent debate and write on tables, their level of enthusiasm for the task increases and the quality of the dialogue and debate will be much higher than asking them to discuss the same point in pairs.

After each group has worked their way round the table, ask each group to then read their original sheet and rank 1, 2 and 3 of what they think is the most important comment on the sheet to the third most important comment. This will then allow you to speed up feedback about the sheets as you can ask groups for their top comment or their third comment etc. Ranking is also a sophisticated skill as the students need to justify their reasoning.

You could extend this task even further by asking the students to swap their sheets and see whether another group agrees with their ranking before you ask for class feedback. By this time, most of the learning has taken place as the students have demonstrated their knowledge and justified their opinions. Hearing class feedback is only for confirmation that they are on the right lines with their thoughts and opinions and should not take very long.

3) Lucky Dip is a starter activity that encourages curiosity from the students. In a dark coloured bag that is not too big, place objects that are related strongly and less strongly to the learning objective of the lesson. For example, if teaching a lesson about connectives then you could bring in objects that offer connections – some more obvious than others. A set of car keys; batteries; a personal item that connects you to someone; a mirror (as it allows you to connect with your present as it shows you who you are now). Ask for volunteers to remove one of the items and ask them a series of questions about the items and see whether eventually the word 'connection' is mentioned. Then, link it to the word connective and therefore the purpose of a 'connective.'

4) You can begin a starter activity with 'If (name of character) was an object, what sort of object would he/she be?' Ask the students to think of ideas in pairs and then share them with another pair and agree the best one that could be shared with the rest of the class. Ask the groups to justify their views, i.e. they need to be able to list three features of the object that make it appropriate for it to be linked to the named character.

5) A visual way of helping students to learn quotes is to use visual drawings such as in Pictionary as this can help the students to understand and retain information. For example:

_____

READING
_____

Reading between the lines

Give students some specific quotations from key extracts from the texts and ask them to change into either word images or actual pictures. An example, from *Romeo and Juliet* by William Shakespeare, would be:

O Romeo, Romeo,
wherefore art thou Romeo?

- Iconic picture of Rome + eo
- Picture of map with a pin in it +
- Picture of number 4
- Picture of artist type paint brushes
- Picture of the Ten Commandments
- Iconic picture of Rome + eo

Students have to design visual words or images for their allocated quotations within a designated time period. You could then take a photograph of each of their visual quotations and upload them onto PowerPoint to create a visual display. The whole class has to work out the quotations based on the visual clues as the PowerPoint is displayed to them. If the presentation looks successful then you could print it out for a future lesson so that all students can refer to it as a tool for learning key quotes.

These starter activities have an English focus and are also focusing on some of the key skills that will be needed in the new English specifications, e.g. developing memory techniques to learn key quotes. However, the starter activity does need to link to the learning and the outcomes of the lesson unlike the bell work activity. Therefore, when choosing a starter activity, it is important to ask 'will this activity demonstrate any new learning from the students?'

Review

This chapter has focused on a range of strategies that can be used at the start of a lesson. The purpose of using bell work activities is essentially about establishing the right behaviour for learning and create a degree of curiosity so that extended learning can take place throughout the rest of the lesson.

The introduction of learning outcomes is key to an outstanding lesson and being able to share the learning that should take place by the end of the lesson is essential.

A few starter activities have been outlined and the main assessment focus of any chosen starter activity should be: Will the students gain new knowledge from completing the starter activity? Will it challenge the students' thinking in any way?

Summary: start of the lesson

There are lots of different ways in which you can begin your lesson and outstanding teachers vary their methods. Imagine being a pupil going from one lesson to the next. If they are all the same we soon disengage. Adding variety makes pupils interested in learning as they never know quite what to expect. Some examples of the start of the lesson include:

Bell work (two minutes)
Share learning outcomes (two minutes)
Big Question (one minute)
Starter activity (five minutes)
Review (two minutes)
  Total: 12 minutes

Share learning outcomes (two minutes)
Big Question (three minutes)
Starter activity (five minutes)
Review (two minutes)
  Total: 12 minutes

Big Question (five minutes)
Learning outcomes (two minutes)
Starter activity (five minutes)
Review (two minutes)
  Total: 14 minutes

Learning outcomes (two minutes)
Big Question (five minutes)
  Total: 7 minutes

(Source: Bartlett, 2014)

Reference

Bartlett, J. (2014) *Becoming an Outstanding Mathematics Teacher*, London: Routledge.

CHAPTER 3

Learning in the main

This stage of the lesson is where the most amount of learning by the students takes place. The students are now aware of where they are heading and what they will be learning. Sharing outcomes is key in helping the students to 'buy in' to the learning. As teachers, we feel more focused if we are told at the start of meetings or a training session what the main aim of the session will be and what information we should leave with. Therefore, if you have successfully set up the introduction to the lesson then this stage will be much easier to plan and share with the students.

When planning this stage of the lesson, it might be helpful to ask 'what will the students know when they leave the classroom that they didn't know when they entered it?' However, how are you going to present this information to the students? How long are the activities going to be? How are you going to know that they have learned anything from them? Are there some key questions that need to be answered? Do you need to share success criteria with the students? How are the students going to be grouped during the lesson? Outstanding teachers are able to plan for these areas but then facilitate the learning by adapting to the needs of the students as the lesson progresses. Outstanding teachers can 'read' a class and the level of engagement of the students.

Listening to the noise level of students is a good indication of when an activity needs to be stopped or explained again. Outstanding teachers can hear the 'key change' as in a piece of music and use that as the sign that they need to intervene in some way. Equally, if there is no 'key change' then they know that the activity might need to be extended longer than they had originally planned as it is apparently more challenging than they had thought.

Being a 'lighthouse' in the classroom and scanning the students is also another strategy that outstanding teachers use. Standing to one side of the classroom and looking at the students, observing what the class looks and sounds like when the students are engaged in learning is also an important part of being an outstanding teacher. It is too easy to think that intervening with individual students is one of the key ways to ensure that learning is taking place. However, it can be just as important to stand back and scan the students and work out where your intervention might be best placed to help facilitate the learning for all students.

Another strategy is to tell the students that you will not answer any questions for the first three minutes after you have set up a learning activity. This allows the students to filter their own problems and hopefully solve them. It also enables you to adopt the 'lighthouse' and see where the lack of a pen is hindering a student from starting their learning or to observe which student appears to have a genuine misunderstanding or challenge with the task. You are then able to place a few pens on the tables where they are needed and move swiftly to the students who clearly need assistance to start their learning. This kind of targeted intervention ensures that outstanding teachers use their time and give their expertise to those who need it to make progress.

Sequencing the learning

One of the most enjoyable features of teaching English is that you don't have to always teach ideas in a linear fashion within a lesson. In English it is possible to start with a conclusion about something and then work with the students to identify whether they agree with the final statement about a character; definition or use of a linguistic device; meaning of a poem etc.

A successful strategy in engaging students with their learning is to ask them to complete the key task of the lesson at the start of this main section of the lesson. For example, if the assessment for a particular scheme of work is that the students need to write an essay comparing two poems then give them four to five minutes at the start of a lesson to attempt to write the plan for their essay. This should be done before there is much teaching from you about how to write essays and compare ideas etc. Clearly, you will have taught the poems in a previous lesson but students should try writing the plan of an essay at the start.

See what the students can do with minimal help. You may wish to put some key words on the board to help some students but see if they can 'struggle' with the planning for just a very short time. Ask the students to think about other subjects and how they write essays, encourage them to use their existing knowledge to see what they can do.

You then show them the brilliant outcome of what you were looking for – a section of a comparative essay that contains all the elements that you wanted them to include. Then take the students through the example and discuss with them what different features are contained in the exemplar. You can ask the students to annotate or add to their own plan (briefly). Use assessment for learning strategies to identify which features the students did or did not include in their own plan and then teach the students those concepts. Outstanding teachers are able to teach the students what they actually do not know rather than what they think they do not know.

Another example could be as follows:

Teaching students about the use of persuasive techniques
Version 1

1) **Starter** – recall and check prior learning about persuasive techniques, e.g. repetition.

2) Teach new words, e.g. hyperbole.

3) Show video clip of *Dragon's Den*. www.youtube.com/watch?v=hp5gTE9 ZScw – Harry Potter Magic Wand Remote.

4) **Main part of the lesson** – ask students to analyse video clip for successful persuasive techniques.

5) Create a list of all the persuasive techniques that the students have found in the video clip and create success criteria.

6) Ask students to write a short analysis of the video clip, identifying how successful the persuasive strategies are.

7) **Plenary** – peer assessment of each other's paragraph using the success criteria which identifies evidence of learning.

Version 2

1) **Starter** – watch video clip www.youtube.com/watch?v=hp5gTE9ZScw – Harry Potter Magic Wand Remote. Ask students to write down as many persuasive techniques as they can that are used in the video clip.

2) Ask students to share their persuasive techniques on mini-whiteboards.

3) How many did they know?

4) Then teach the missing words, e.g. hyperbole; rhetorical questions; inclusive pronouns, etc.

5) **Main part of the lesson** – Then watch a 'poor' version of a *Dragon's Den* presentation e.g. compu-table www.youtube.com/watch?v=eP9pgUBJRPY

6) Don't tell the students about its quality and ask them to write down as many persuasive techniques as they can. What was the problem? How did they know?

25

7) With the students, create success criteria of how persuasive language should be used.

8) Ask the students to write a short analysis of the Harry Potter video clip identifying how successful the persuasive strategies are, while referring to the success criteria.

9) **Plenary** – peer assessment of each other's paragraph using the success criteria which identifies evidence of learning.

Version 1 is teaching in a linear way and taking the students step by step through the concepts of persuasive techniques. There is nothing wrong with this version but Version 2 presents a slightly different way of presenting the same information to the students. I would suggest that it encourages the students to engage with their learning more as they are demonstrating what they know about persuasive language before taking steps to fill in the 'gaps'.

Sequencing the learning can be about moving the main learning activity of the lesson to as early stage in the lesson as possible. Let the students 'struggle' with their learning slightly and see how far they can get. Then put in place the strategies that are needed to help all the students learn. The students can then revisit their initial attempts towards the end of the lesson and rewrite them or improve them. Doing it this way will also show clear progress as you have taught them only what they need to know.

The main assessment activity

There are a range of activities to engage the students and help them to develop and widen their learning about specific topics. The following might be activities that you wish to include as part of the main assessment activity:

Writing

- RAFT stands for role, audience, format and topic. Students choose a role and then write from that perspective to a specific audience. This encourages the students to demonstrate their understanding of a concept by writing in a different style. It is encouraging them to apply their learning in a different context, moving from surface learning to deeper learning (RAFT is cited in *Classroom Instruction from A–Z* by Barbara Blackburn, p. 175, but she quotes RAFT from Santa, Havens, and Macumber, 1996). (The examples in Table 3.1 are my own.)

Table 3.1 RAFT Grid

Role	Audience	Format	Topic
Semi-colon	GCSE students	5× tweets	How it is used incorrectly
Adjective	Year 2 students	Children's story with only 100 words	Adjectives create an interest in sentences
Noun	Young adults	Blog with links to examples	Different types of nouns and their uses
Questions	Parents	Magazine article about how to question your teenager about their school day	Effect of using interrogative; rhetorical; open and closed questions

- Circle of Ideas – students sometimes find starting a paragraph for an essay or writing in the style of a broadsheet or a magazine article quite difficult if they are asked to do it by themselves. This activity allows them to gain support from their peers.

  All students start with a piece of A3 paper and sit in groups of four. Tell the students the overall task which is that they will be writing an article in a magazine outlining the advantages and disadvantages of teenagers using a mobile phone. However, explain that they are only going to write the first paragraph in this particular task which will be approximately eight lines in length.

  Give students an opportunity to talk to each other about some initial ideas or even brainstorm some advantages and disadvantages in pairs before starting the writing. Then ask students to write down the first two sentences that they would use for their introductory paragraph. Keep the tension of the learning going by having a strict time limit, possibly just over a minute for this task. Then ask the students to pass their piece of paper to the person on their left. Then ask them to write down the second pair of lines in the paragraph which are linked to the first set and so on.

  After three rotations, the students collectively should have written eight lines of four introductory paragraphs in each group. Each student should now have the paragraph that they originally started with.

  You then can ask the students to assess the quality of their paragraph against success criteria which will be discussed in Chapter 6. The students then edit and improve their paragraph accordingly, either in pairs or individually against the success criteria. You could also introduce an exemplar of a successful introductory paragraph at this stage if you wish.

  This strategy allows students to feel supported by their peers and gain expertise from them in a non-threatening and supportive way while ensuring that it adheres to the success criteria.

Reading

- The concept of Thinking Hats was created by Edward de Bono in *Six Thinking Hats* (1999). It is a strategy that encourages human thinking to be creative but structured at the same time. It is used by the corporate and educational world as a tool to develop ideas and responses in a clear manner.

  The concept of the Six Thinking Hats is that it encourages the students to filter their thinking in a specific way. It forces them to think in ways that might not be familiar to them and it encourages them to widen their thinking and reaction to specific ideas.

  This is a link to a YouTube video about the Six Thinking Hats. www.youtube.com/watch?v=UjSjZOjNIJg. You also find many other resources on the internet but for copyright reasons they will not be listed here.

  The Six Thinking Hats can be used as a resource in many ways to structure thinking in the English classroom. I have provided an example in Table 3.2 about how to use it to structure thinking about a novel.

Table 3.2 Six Thinking Hats

Blue Hat	This is the hat that can control the use of the thinking hats but also can be the one that helps to summarise the thinking that is taking place. In a classroom context, it can be a teacher but doesn't have to be.
White Hat: facts and figures	What is the title of the book? Who is the author? When was it published? Has it won any awards? What is the outline of the plot? What are the character names? Where and when is the novel set?
Red Hat: emotions and feelings	Did you like the book? Why or why not? Were there any sections that made you laugh or feel sad? Do you like (name of character)? Why or why not? How did you feel about (insert reference to section of novel)? How did you feel about the ending of the novel? Do you think (name of character) was treated fairly?
Black Hat: cautious and careful	Do you think (name of character) could have reacted to (name of incident) in a different way? What problems could have been avoided if the character had behaved differently? Does this novel or character remind you of anything else?
Yellow Hat: positive	What was the advantage of setting the novel in the place that the author did? What was positive about the main character's age? How well do you think the character solved the problem of ...? How successful was the heroine of the novel?
Green Hat: creative	What would happen if the ending was different? How else could the heroine have reacted to a (named) situation? What would happen if the novel was set in the twenty-first century? What would change?

Thinking Hats is a strategy that can be used in lots of different contexts that are too numerous to list here. However, there are resources on the TES about using the Thinking Hats in an English context.

It can also be used to help behaviour for learning by encouraging the students to react and think through their reaction to a task. For example, having to write yet another essay or learn more quotes for their exam. Working through the thinking styles allows the students to let off steam (Red Hat) but also helps them to understand the reasons and the importance of the tasks they have been set (White Hat). It can also encourage the students to share ideas about how they would like to learn the quotes for the closed book exam (Green Hat), which perhaps you might not have thought about.

- Conscience Alley – this is essentially a drama activity but it encourages the students to think about a concept or an issue from a novel in a different way.

  Students will be the 'conscience' of a key character in a novel or a poem and they are going to give different perspectives of what is going on inside a character's head.

  For example, ask for a volunteer to be Juliet. The class divides into two lines facing each other, quite close to each other. 'Juliet' then walks down the alley walking towards the poison at the end of the lines. She pauses alongside each student so that they can quietly voice her thoughts. One side would give the reasons she should take the poison; the other would give reasons why she should not take the poison. Each side takes it in turn to speak. Juliet would hear one positive reason and then a negative one. Juliet can then state which side she found the most convincing once she reaches the end of the line and a class discussion can take place about this. It can take two or three times of practice before the class gets the hang of it and makes it sound convincing.

  You may also find that the students need to be in groups first to brainstorm some things that they might say to Juliet. It is a very effective way of adding visualisation and dramatising the thoughts and ideas of a character. A simple prop such as a small bottle for this particular example, placed at the end of the line, can really help with the authenticity of this task. The activity doesn't take too much space as it can be done at the front of the classroom with hopefully just the first line of desks slightly pushed back.

- Role on the Wall is another strategy of doing a character study. Divide the class into pairs and give each pair a piece of A3 paper. This can be done on the floor with much bigger pieces of paper if you wish to create a display from it.

○ Students will have been reading a novel and discussed the actions and language of a character. For this task, ask them to draw the shape of gingerbread man with fat arms and legs. However, there needs to be space around the edge of the paper for writing too. Then ask the students to write down adjectives that could be used to describe the characteristics of the character that the reader sees inside the gingerbread man shape. Ask them to provide page numbers for quotations to support their ideas.

○ The next stage is for the students to write down on the outside of the gingerbread man adjectives that describe the character as other characters see him/her. Again, the students need to provide evidence of this by using page numbers.

○ The students then swap Role on the Walls and add to and improve each others' ideas. This can be repeated a few times as well.

○ What is written inside and outside the gingerbread man can also change as you may wish adjectives to be written down inside the gingerbread man about what the character is thinking in their own head, etc.

○ You could then photograph the Roles on the Wall to create a display for the students or to create a collage for them to revise from. Alternatively, you could do this on a bigger scale and have the whole class involved in creating a larger Role on the Wall which is again photographed to share with the students to help them with the revision of key quotes.

Teaching poetry

• Teaching poetry to students can be dull and repetitive. There is a strong focus on poetry in the new English specifications so the need for creative ways to interest students in poetry is not going to go away.

○ Unrolling a poem can be a useful way of modelling to students about how they can develop their own personal response to it which will be an essential skill to use in the unseen poetry unit in some of the new exam specifications.

Put a poem that the students have not seen before into PowerPoint and then animate each line so one line appears at a time at each click of the mouse. Ask the students to share their reactions about each line with you or ask them to discuss it in pairs first etc. Outstanding teachers will prepare the questions in advance to ensure that the ones that the students are asked are a combination of low order and high order questions. This activity is very teacher led so probably only works for one or two stanzas but it allows the students to build up their confidence about how to develop their own personal responses.

○ Working in groups on poems can be a method to help engage the interest in the poem. However, this group strategy can also ensure there is individual accountability within this group work task if you give each member of the group a different colour pen. You may wish to read the poem to the students first before they start this activity to ensure that they have a very general overview of its meaning and are not struggling with misinterpretations of words etc.

○ Divide the class into the same number of groups as there are stanzas in a poem that they have not seen before. Each group is given a copy of a stanza glued onto an A3 piece of paper so that there is room to write around it.

○ Ask the group to read their stanza and then write down five questions that they have about that stanza. Encourage the students to ask questions about topic; rhyming patterns; poetic techniques; language used. In summary, interpretation; language; structure and personal response. If using different colour pens for each group then students can write down one question and you can easily assess the quality and contribution of each student by the colour of the pen that they are using. Keep the time limit for this task quite short so it gives the students a healthy tension for the activity, possibly four to five minutes.

○ Ask students to pass their copy of the poem to the group on their left. Ask the groups to now work out which are the best three questions that have been written down. Ask them to cross out the two least successful questions. This task should only take about two minutes.

○ Ask the group to then pass on the copy of the poem again. Now the students are faced with a different stanza but have essentially read two other stanzas of the poem. Ask the students to write down the answers to the three questions about the stanza. The students in this group have now become 'experts' about this stanza by what they have written down. Ensure that this group annotates their own copy of this stanza in their anthology as well as they will need to be able to refer to it for the next task.

○ The next stage of the task is to divide the class again so one member of each group now gets together to form a new group. Essentially, use the jigsaw method to group the students again. For example, at the beginning of the task each group was given a stanza so they would have been numbered Group 1, 2, 3, 4 and 5. When you want the students to jigsaw ensure that the new groups have one person from Group 1, one person from Group 2, one person from Group 3 etc. in it. This means that you now have one student in each group who can share ideas about each of the stanzas of the poem.

○ Tell the new groups to share their ideas with each other so that every student in that group has notes about each stanza. This task might take only about seven to eight minutes. The class should now have some notes about the poem in their anthology and they have done all the learning and the activity.

○ You may decide to hear about each stanza from different groups but I would suggest that this is not the most successful strategy to use. It can affect the pace of the lesson and the students have already written down their notes for each stanza so talking about the same points will not help move their learning on. The students have 'struggled' slightly with their learning and now it is time to move them on to the next stage.

○ For the next activity you could put your version of each annotated stanza on the whiteboard and talk the students through it. Why do the students think you have made the notes you have? Why do they think you have annotated certain points? This way the students have a model to work from so you can ensure that they all have good quality notes by the end of the lesson but they have done most of the learning. They have built up their confidence about their own personal responses but have also been supported by seeing a good quality version so that they can improve the types of notes and annotations that they will make in future.

• Another method to use when teaching a poem is to fragment it. Wordle does something similar but it doesn't fragment and list the poem alphabetically in such a way to enable comments to be made about themes; repetition; use of grammatical terms etc. Fragmenting a poem is a tool that can be completed in Word and here is a description of how to do it:

1) Put a poem into Word
2) Select the whole text
3) Go to the **Edit Menu** and select **Find** – could then be another tab that says **Advanced Find and Replace**
4) In the top Find, type a **space** (by pressing the space bar)
5) In the bottom Replace with: type **^p**
6) Click on **Replace All**
7) You will now see your text is a long, single-word column going down the page. Select this long column using **Select All**
8) Next click on **Table** from the main icon bar at the top of the page
9) Next click on **Sort**
10) Click on **Ascending**.

You should end up with a Word document that looks something like this with all the words from the poem in alphabetical order:

a
ahead
and
and
and
and
and
and
as
at
at
away
ballroom
Before
Before
before
before
bend
best
bites
blows
bold
born
bring
clatters
clear
close
corner
could
dance
decade
doesn't
dress

You can then ask the students to analyse the language and poetic features with the words listed like above. Alternatively, you can turn it into a source of words by creating a table for the students to use to write their own poems.

○ You can do this by highlighting the fragmented poem

○ Then select **Table**

○ Select convert **Text to Table** and then select that you want one column and one row. You may then delete all the prepositions so you end up with a table that mainly contains verbs, nouns, adjectives and adverbs. See Table 3.3 for an example that just uses a few words from a poem.

Table 3.3 Make a poem from a Source of Words

ahead   away ballroom   bend   best   bites   blows   bold   born   bring clatters   clear   close corner corner   could dance   decade   doesn't   dress
Choose any words from the list above to make your own poem. Each time you use a word cross it off the list.

These types of activities encourage the students to see the poem in a different format and make judgements about its structure and language use. This can also be used on any other text to encourage a language study of it developing the knowledge of grammatical terms and features. The use of a Source of Words also allows students to become creative with the words used in a poem. These activities work well if the students have not seen the poem before as it is another strategy to help them develop their own personal response and confidence in spotting patterns and structural techniques in poetry.

A key way to engage learners is to give them choice about the activities that they engage in and although that may not always be possible a strategy such as Tic-Tac-Toe can help to give an element of ownership to the students.

• Tic-Tac-Toe is essentially a grid of activities and the students have to choose a range of activities that follows the form of a traditional line of noughts or crosses. This task may be appropriate for a whole scheme of work or for a few assessment activities. It allows the activities to be differentiated and provide a challenge for all, as one row can be less difficult than another row, and the students have to choose whichever ones they wish but have to create a straight or diagonal line through the grid. See Table 3.4 as an example that would be based on studying a novel but I have not related it to a specific one which is why no character name is mentioned.

Table 3.4 Tic-Tac-Toe activities

Locate eight key quotations from pp. 114–118 and explain what words present the reader with a view of the character.	Write four Facebook entries about the key character. Have to be approximately 50 words each and have to use words from the quotes on pp. 114–118 to demonstrate knowledge of the character's attitude and behaviour.	Write a letter to the father of the main character. This letter needs to be written from the perspective of the hero as he outlines all his key characteristics and virtues. Letter should be no more than 200 words and should list the characteristics that you can find on pp. 114–118.
Write a play script of 300 words between the three key characters of the novel showing how you think they would still react if the novel hadn't ended where it had. Remember to base their actions and words on evidence from the text.	Complete a Role on the Wall for the three key characters. Include what the reader thinks of the characters and what other characters think of the three key characters. Remember to use quotations as evidence.	Write a newspaper article in the style of a tabloid article about the behaviour and actions of the three key characters. Think about what the paper would report that they were doing, where they would go and comments that they would give to the reporter. Make sure you base it on evidence from the text.
Write an essay comparing the key two characters of the novel. What are their positive features? What are their negative features? Do they share any characteristics? Which ones? Refer to A01 and A03 in your writing. Use key quotations to support your comparison.	Write an essay about How far do you think that (name of main character) was to blame for the murder of (name of another character)? Refer to A01 and A03 in your writing. Use key quotations from the chapters we have studied.	Look at the extract on page 117 and write about its importance in the novel. What does it tell us about the key characters? What does it tell us about the future plot? What does it tell us about the attitudes of the time? How do we as readers react to this incident? Refer to A01 and A03 in your writing. Use quotations to support your comments.

All of the above activities need a form of assessment at the end to assess the students' knowledge and understanding. All main activities need a progress check after each one and this can be done in a variety of ways. This will be covered more in Chapter 6, How do I know?

Summary

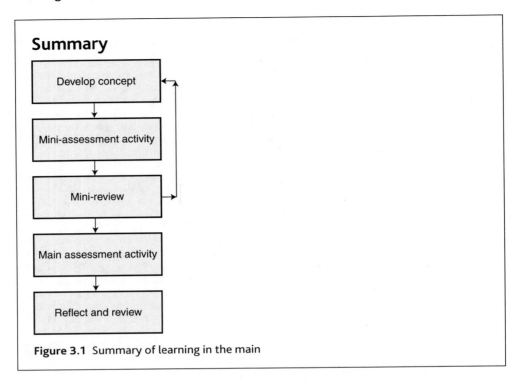

Figure 3.1 Summary of learning in the main

References

Blackburn, B. (2016) *Classroom Instruction from A–Z*, Second Edition, New York: Routledge.

De Bono, E. (1999) *Six Thinking Hats*, London: Penguin.

Gilbert, I. (2007) *The Little Book of Thunks: 260 Questions to Make Your Brain Go Ouch!* Carmarthen: Crown House Publishing.

Ginnis, P. (2002) *The Teacher's Toolkit: Raise Classroom Achievement with Strategies for Every Learner*, Carmarthen: Crown House Publishing.

So how does it all end?

An outstanding lesson should demonstrate that students have all made exceptional progress. However, this is only possible to reliably ascertain if at the beginning of the lesson the existing learning has been checked. An outstanding teacher is then able to adapt their planned lesson based on the information gained at the start of the lesson. The same is true for the end of the lesson – an outstanding teacher will use it as an opportunity to gain real knowledge about what the students have learned and then use this for planning the next lesson.

The plenary is the time to ask the question 'what have the students learned?' That is not the same as what 'have the students *done*?' during the lesson but what have they actually *learned*? The plenary then requires clear planning; an outstanding teacher is able to design activities that check the actual knowledge in the room. This may not be what the teacher would expect all the students to have learned but what the students actually demonstrate they know by the end of the lesson.

Learning outcomes

The plenary is the stage of the lesson where you need to return to the learning outcomes and by various strategies ascertain how far the students have achieved their learning outcomes – not to ascertain how much of the task the students have completed but actually how much have they learned.

This is where using Paul Ginnis' differentiated learning outcomes is helpful, as the ones that were used in an example in Chapter 2 (see page 12) – define, analyse and compare – are assessable. It is possible to take in the students' books and see and assess whether they have been able to define, analyse and compare.

Another strategy would be to ask the students to determine their own assessment of their completion of the outcomes. One way to do this is at the end of the lesson to ask the students to put their exercise books in different coloured trays:

- green = 'yes I have completed my outcome';
- orange = 'I have completed most of the outcome but not as detailed as it could be';
- red = 'I have not completed my outcome for various reasons and I need help or further guidance'.

These definitions can be presented to the students on the whiteboard and then trays can just have coloured paper stuck to the top of them indicating which is which. Students are assessing their own progress when they place their exercise books in the trays but it also has a further benefit as it can help you with marking too. It can give you a guide about which books might need more detailed marking or time spent on them due to the fact that the students felt that they had not achieved their outcome. More importantly, it also gives you a quick indication of where the learning is more and less secure and can help you with planning for the next lesson.

When giving the books back to the students at the start of a future lesson, you could display the names of the students on the whiteboard in columns in the colours green, orange and red, matching the ones they selected when they handed in their books. At this point, you can choose to comment verbally on the accuracy of the students' assessment of their completion of the outcomes. You could do this by moving the names of the students out of one column and placing them into another one, e.g. moving from red to orange. Demonstrating progress in this way can help the students gain confidence in their own self assessment against their chosen outcome and you are also giving them feedback about their learning.

Brilliant outcome

At the start of the lesson, you may have shared the brilliant outcome with the students if you thought it was appropriate to your lesson as discussed in Chapter 2. You may have asked the students to assess themselves against the continuum line towards this brilliant outcome. For example, the brilliant outcome when teaching poetry at KS4 might be 'to evaluate a poem with a critical and well structured argument supported by detailed and personalised analysis of the language of the poem and by excellent use of poetic terms'.

You can now return to the continuum line and ask students to assess themselves and decide whether they are any closer to reaching the brilliant outcome that is taken from one of the highest level grade descriptors at KS4. However, an outstanding teacher will know that it is not enough just to let the students state a number. Further questions need to be asked of the students to help them justify their assessment.

- What is it that they learned today that has helped them move closer to the brilliant outcome?

- What did they do today that helped them learn and move towards the brilliant outcome? e.g. contribute to discussions; demonstrate positive behaviour for learning; annotate their text in detail; answer teacher led questions successfully; ask relevant and insightful questions during the lesson.

- What did you (the teacher) do to help them move towards the brilliant outcome?

- Can they articulate what next steps they need to take in future lessons to achieve the brilliant outcome?

A brilliant outcome such as the one outlined above is not going to be achieved in one lesson; a series of lessons will gradually move the students towards it and you may find that it is easier to introduce other outcomes that are more obtainable within a lesson but always linking it to the brilliant learning outcome.

It is not always possible to ask every student these questions due to lack of time and also it can affect the pace of the lesson. As an outstanding teacher you may find it more appropriate to question representatives of students from various groups within your class (see below for further explanation).

Big Question

In Chapter 2 we introduced the idea of the Big Question. An example of a Big Question might be 'Do you like or dislike Atticus in to *To Kill A Mockingbird*? Why?' It was suggested that students put their initial answer to the Big Question in an envelope that can be opened during this plenary stage of the lesson or at other progress check points. Students can be asked to open their envelopes in the plenary and discuss in pairs how their point of view has changed from the start of the lesson to this stage.

You could ask to hear comments from the students about how their initial answers have changed. After time for paired discussion, questions by the teacher should be aimed at representatives of the various groups within the class, whether that be low, medium or high ability, pupil premium or students with special educational needs. Using whichever method your school uses to group their students provides you with the opportunity to ask targeted questions to students who represent those groups in your classroom. Asking a combination of high order and lower order questions of the different representatives of the various groups for this type of plenary will help you to gauge the progress of a range of students.

So how does it all end?

For example, some of the questions about Atticus might be:

- What does Atticus do that we as a reader see as being positive?
- What does Atticus do that we as a reader see as being harsh or negative?
- Whose viewpoint is the book written from? Who is the narrator?
- How might we as a reader be affected by the narrator's viewpoint?
- What issues could be missing from the character view that we have of Atticus? What is Scout likely to have focused on or missed out?
- What evidence in the novel do you have to support your viewpoint?

Plenary activities

There are some stand alone plenary activities that can be adapted to your specific lesson to ascertain the depth and quality of the new learning of the students and these are described here:

- 3-2-1 – students write down on a whiteboard or piece of paper or articulate to you *three* pieces of new knowledge that they have learned; *two* answers to questions that helped them learn or two questions that they would like to have answered next lesson; *one* target that they are going to set themselves for future lessons. The content of 3-2-1 is interchangeable and can be adapted to whatever works for the information that you wish to gain from the students.

  For example, 3-2-1 after a poetry lesson might be:
  ○ *three* poetic techniques that they have been taught during the lesson;
  ○ *two* questions that helped them to learn, which might have been – Where is this poem set? Who is the poet's voice in the poem?;
  ○ *one* target that they might set themselves, which could be – to be able to locate key quotes and analyse the importance of individual words within the quotes and also use poetic terminology in answer.

- Exit Tickets can be an extension of 3-2-1 as you could create an Exit Ticket around the structure of 3-2-1 as the students have to hand in an Exit Ticket. However, an outstanding use of an Exit Ticket is to ask the students to write something down that demonstrates their new knowledge.

  For example, ask the students to:
  ○ summarise the use of new linguistic terms;
  ○ assess the impact of poetic terms in a poem they have studied;
  ○ write their personal response to a poem;
  ○ write down the four key features of writing a successful argument.

The Exit Ticket should encourage the students to write less than fifty words, as being succinct also ensures that the students are confident enough in their new knowledge that they can summarise it. Students need to put their name on the Exit Ticket and then hand it in to you at the end of the lesson. You can use this information to ascertain how secure the students' new knowledge is by the quality of their answers and then plan for the next lesson as appropriate.

- Another plenary technique is to use progress charts. Students fill in a small progress chart to indicate their current level of understanding about a certain topic at the start, middle and end of a lesson. This can be created as shown in Table 4.1, where '1' represents least understanding and '5' represents most.

Table 4.1 Progress chart

5				
4				
3				
2				
1				
	Start of the lesson	First progress check	Second progress check	End of the lesson

Students colour in the boxes to indicate their current or increasing level of understanding. This can even be done on a mini-whiteboard as they can quickly draw this table or show you the number to demonstrate their level of understanding. You can allocate descriptors of level of knowledge or understanding for each of the numbers on the progress chart. You may wish take them from the language used in the Assessment Objectives in the exam specifications. For example, these progress checks can become more useful if the numbers are not just described as very secure; secure; struggling; don't understand as these terms can be quite subjective. Linking these numbers to something assessable such as Assessment Objectives within a scheme of work or exam specification can help to make them more measurable and the students more accountable.

I have used the terms first progress check etc. but with no timings as that depends on the complexity of what you are teaching to the students. Some teachers think that students' progress should be checked after each fifteen minutes but the topic of the lesson; time of the lesson; type of group etc. can have a huge impact on how quickly learning can be ascertained. Therefore, I have deliberately not put in timings. However, self assessment by the students of these progress checks needs to be moderated with questions:
- Why have they assessed themselves against that number?
- How do they know that their knowledge has improved?
- What have they done to demonstrate that increase?

So how does it all end?

You can then check these progress checks if they are left out on tables as the lesson progresses. Additionally, you then can take in these progress checks at the end of the lesson especially if you leave space at the bottom for the students to complete a reflective sentence such as 'I did well because I can demonstrate ....'

- The quiz is a task that was discussed in Chapter 2. This stage of the lesson is the time to repeat the quiz and see whether the students can answer more questions than they could before. In Chapter 2, we outlined that it was important to include questions that the students couldn't answer at the start of the lesson. Therefore, the plenary can be used as the time to ascertain whether new learning has taken place by seeing whether the students can answer more of the questions.

  It might seem obvious but it is imperative that clear behaviour for learning strategies is used at this stage of the lesson in order that you can gauge the learning of all students. There should be limited opportunities for the students to simply copy the answers of the students who are sitting near them. For example, if you are using mini-whiteboards to gain this information then you need to have a clear rule that no one raises their whiteboard until they hear the countdown of '3, 2, 1 – show me'. This allows all students to demonstrate their knowledge to you simultaneously. It was suggested in Chapter 2 that you could take a photo of the students at the start of the lesson with their answers to the quiz. You could now display this photo on the whiteboard and use it as a reference to discuss with the students who has gained new knowledge and who has not. Why and why not?

- Another plenary is to use true/false cards. These can be easily created on pieces of paper that can say 'true' on one side and 'false' on the other. They can be laminated for future use. This method assesses mainly the recall memory of students. However, with the new specifications and the need for the students to learn quotes and order of plot sequences then it does have a place as a plenary activity.

  ○ You can pose questions to students in which they have to answer 'true' or 'false'. This is a very good way of ascertaining their recognition of quotes or plot structure. You can put examples of quotations from texts that are slightly wrong and ask them to indicate whether they are true or false; you can put page numbers of quotations and ask whether they are true or false; you can bullet point a sequence to a plot and ask whether it is true or false.

○ As suggested earlier, this task needs clear rules and routines of behaviour of learning and follow-up questions need to be asked too. Why is the sequence of the plot wrong? What is wrong with the quotation? Again, asking these questions to specific students will enable you to assess the learning of different groups in your classroom.

Reflection

It is important to encourage students to reflect on their own progress and also to start to develop their own targets. However, this can only be meaningfully done if the students have clear learning outcomes to assess themselves against and also know where they are going in future lessons. When asked to set themselves targets, too many students simply put that they need to 'write more' or 'improve the detail of their answers' or even 'write neater'. These are not the types of targets that we wish them to develop as a reflective learner. Therefore, the Assessment Objectives of the exam specification or the scheme of work, learning outcomes or the brilliant outcome need to be shared with the students at the end of the lesson to encourage them to be able to assess their own learning and set targets in a reflective but meaningful manner.

Some of the following strategies might help your students to become more reflective about their progress:

• In Chapter 2, we introduced the KWL Grid (see page 18) and the plenary is the stage of the lesson where you ask the students to reflect on their learning and write down what they think they have learned in your lesson under the L column (learning). You could give them a structure to use to fill in the L column. For example, some sentence starters to encourage reflection could be 'The new knowledge I have learned today is …', 'I have learned something new today because I can … and at the start of the lesson I could only …'.

The KWL Grid can be taken in at the end of the lesson and you can use this information to ascertain whether knowledge of the students is secure or not. You can also write a comment on the bottom of the KWL Grid to suggest a new target for future lessons. Students will not engage with reflective activities about their learning unless they feel that you have read or reacted to their reflections in some way.

Sometimes, just giving the class two or three targets based on the information gained from KWL Grids is sufficient. To be an outstanding teacher, there is no need to mark and write something down on every student's grid. Outline two or three targets for the class and make sure they are colour coded against the colours of Post-it notes that you have. Ask the students to select their Post-it note according to the colour of the target that they are going to set themselves. Tell them to leave this Post-it note on the corner of the desk throughout the lesson. You can then assess whether their chosen target is appropriate or not and intervene as you see fit.

Then at the end of this lesson ask them to write down their progress against their new target which was taken from the information you gained from the KWL Grid from the previous lesson. This Post-it note, if dated, can then be stuck onto the KWL Grid and this pattern can be repeated for a few more lessons while on the same topic. I would suggest that at the end of the lessons on a specific topic, you take a photo of the KWL Grids with the dated Post-it notes on them – probably three or four Post-it notes would be sufficient. Then print out the photos and use them to form part of the data that you are collating to demonstrate the progress of your students.

- Another reflective strategy is to use 'two stars and a wish' which is a common self or peer assessment tool. However, it can be used equally well as a structure for the students to reflect on their progress in a lesson. You can create a small sheet like an Exit Ticket for the two stars and a wish or ask the students to write it down in their exercise books. Two stars for two things that they have learned and a wish for a target that they need to set themselves when assessed against the learning outcomes or the brilliant outcome.

- Using the acronym of SIR at the end of students' work can also be another way of encouraging students to reflect on their writing. S = success; I = improvement and R = reflection. Again, ticket type pieces of paper can be made for the students or alternatively they can copy this down into their book leaving about three to four lines for the comments.

The SIR structure can be used in different ways. You can mark the students' work and write comments for the success and improvement sections. Once the students have read your comment they can then write their own reflection about the targets that they need to set.

Alternatively, students can assess their own work against a clear success criterion (in Chapter 6) and write a comment under success and improvement. You can write a comment under reflection and set them a target.

When asking students to write their own targets as in the SIR structure it can be easier to list a few on the board and ask them to choose their targets from this list. This can then avoid the types of pointless targets that I have already explained. With the demise of national levels, asking students to set their own targets against the criteria that you are using in your own school will become more important. The SIR acronym gives you a structure to enable you to encourage your students to do this.

Another suggestion would be to build up photographic evidence of how the use of the SIR structure is improving the quality of the students' work. Taking a photo of the SIR comments and then the subsequent piece of work where the targets have been addressed will again provide you with undeniable evidence of the progress that your students are making. This can be shared with parents and senior staff and can complement or start to replace your use of a mark book or tracking sheet.

Home learning

Homework that is meaningful and deepens learning for students has now become a focus for Ofsted. *Inspection Handbook* (September 2015) states that teaching that has been rated as outstanding in a school needs to demonstrate that 'Teachers set challenging homework, in line with the school's policy and as appropriate for the age and stage of pupils, that consolidates learning, deepens understanding and prepares pupils very well for work to come'.

Homework is not popular with students for many reasons but lack of choice can be a key reason for lack of engagement with it. Some strategies here may help to stimulate some creative ideas for developing homework within your classroom.

- Take away homework is a structure that contains generic homework tasks that the students are allocated on a random basis. Ross McGill has written about it http://teachertoolkit.me/2014/01/28/takeawayhmk-is-unhomework/ and includes links to other teachers who have successfully used this strategy. It is similar to the Tic-Tac-Toe structure that was discussed in Chapter 3 (see page 34). You create a significant number of homework tasks for each year group/key stage as a department which are displayed at all times in your classroom. The students are allotted them on a weekly basis or can choose one if you wish. The homework tasks need to be simple and clear so that the students can write them down and 'take them away'.

  Students can be presented these tasks in the style of a take away pizza menu and the students are encouraged to tick off when they have completed them. This way it is used as a tracking tool that can be kept in the students' books or can be kept as an electronic document. Creating take away homework also means that it can easily be shared with parents on the school website or sent home in paper form. Parents can then engage with their children about their homework when they are told that their son or daughter has take away homework.

So how does it all end?

- Another strategy for involving parents in the completion of their child's homework is to use 'Ask me what I have learned today?' This encourages parents to question their child about the learning that has taken place in the lesson that day. However, this needs support for the parents and this can be done by the school website.
  - ○ For example, if new poetic terms have been learned then that list can be displayed on the parents' section of the website and parents can use it as reference when talking to their child about the poetic terms.
  - ○ A plot summary of a new novel that the students have learned could be displayed in the same way and again prompt questions given to the parents.
  - ○ Linguistic terms or key quotes that students need to learn could be displayed on the school website for parents to use to test their child.
  - ○ Depending on the complexity of the website, parents could be given answers to a quiz about specific knowledge that they could use to test their child. To avoid the students having access to the answers the document could be emailed directly to the parent.

This parental involvement through the school website should not make too much extra work for you as the documents about the plot summary, quiz questions and linguistic terminology would all be ones that you had created for the lesson. The only extra work would be uploading it to the website or emailing it to the parents. However, the time spent doing this will inevitably pay off with parental involvement in their child's education which can only be a positive thing.

- 'Questions for the future' is another homework activity that can help the students to develop their knowledge. However, it requires that the students have some understanding of the content or at least the objective and maybe some of the outcomes of their future lesson. The homework can be for the students to ask a specified number of questions about a topic. For example, if their next topic is 'how to write an argument' then ask the students to write down three questions for homework about what they would like answered by the end of their next lesson. For example, what is the structure for writing an argument?

  You can use these questions as a starter for your next lesson. Ask the students to share their questions with their partner at the start of the lesson. Ask the partner to highlight the best question of the three and cross out the other two. Return the questions to the original student and then this student writes their one question down on a mini-whiteboard. Ask the students to hold up their whiteboards and then you take a photo of the whole class.

Part of the plenary for this lesson could be to display the photo on the whiteboard. Then you refer to all the questions that are on the mini-whiteboards in the photo and see whether you have covered all the students' questions. Using a photo in this way can be more successful than using Post-it notes as it is easier to see which questions came from which students. This can allow you to differentiate the discussion; target questions at specific students in order to assess the depth of their knowledge on the topic.

- Another homework strategy is to use blogs as a tool for reflection. There are many different types of blogs that can be used in an educational context but GoogleDocs, although not necessarily a blog, does allow documents to be shared within a class. Some of the reflective tasks that have been discussed earlier in this chapter could be transferred to a blog/shared document that the students have to contribute to on a regular basis which you can easily monitor and respond to.

- Twitter can also be used for homework which can complement the blog/shared documents. This is probably more suitable for sixth form students. It is possible to set up a Twitter account that you can lock so that followers have to request to follow you. For example, this means that you can create a Twitter account that only has your sixth form students as your followers. Set it up so you follow the appropriate people who are going to extend the depth and breadth of your sixth formers' knowledge. For their homework, ask them to write a blog/shared document with their feedback/comments about a particular article or item that has been posted on that Twitter account in the last five days. Again, this can prove to be a very stimulating and interesting way to start your next lesson as you can access their documents and create an interesting debate about various topical issues that they may not normally read or engage with.

So how does it all end?

Summary

The final stage of the lesson, whether it is called a plenary or not, should check the learning of the students within that specific lesson. The progress of the learning may not cover all of the learning outcomes presented at the start of the lesson, as it is now understood that sustained learning takes place over time.

A plenary is about feedback. By doing the type of plenary tasks in this chapter, you are gaining feedback about the learning but also your teaching. Students are providing you with information about what you need to do more of or less of in the next lesson so you can then adapt your teaching accordingly.

A successful plenary will tell you as the teacher what learning has taken place in any one lesson. It will provide you with information about what needs to be learned in future lessons to achieve the agreed outcomes and objectives.

CHAPTER 5

What's in a question?

Questions in either written or verbal form are an important method for you to ascertain what students' current knowledge is or whether they have learned any new information at various stages of the lesson.

There are lots of books about using questioning strategies in the classroom and as teachers of English, I think we would all agree that using questions is one of the most dynamic and interesting strategies that we ever use to teach our subject. Therefore, as an outstanding teacher it is essential to know how to use a range of them in one lesson. You might need to 'mix' up your strategies in order to elicit a range of information from students as well as create an interesting and engaging debate on a certain topic. Some of the most exciting English lessons that I have ever taught were ones where an answer to a question from a student meant that for a short time, as a class, we discussed a view or an idea that was unexpected. I reacted to an answer from a student and we explored that idea in full by asking questions of each other and encouraging all to respond to answers and engage in a discussion, explaining their point of view. This 'unexpected' moment is always one of the memorable ones in any English teacher's classroom.

Learning outcomes as questions

Learning outcomes have been discussed in Chapter 2 and how they differ from a learning objective. I outlined the idea of using Paul Ginnis' adaptation of Bloom's Taxonomy to create learning outcomes as they are assessable.

Another way of introducing learning outcomes is to present them as questions to students. The learning outcomes can still be structured around Paul Ginnis' points but are presented as questions instead. Using outcomes in this way helps you to immediately assess the knowledge in the room and, if the students can all answer the three questions that you have posed, you know that your lesson is going to have to be adapted immediately. Alternatively, if they can't answer any of the questions, then you know that you are going to have to repeat much of the information in various ways in the lesson giving the students the opportunity to read, write and speak about the new knowledge that you are presenting to them.

If we return to the learning outcomes on *Pride and Prejudice* that were discussed in Chapter 2 as it is easier for comparison to see how they can be turned into questions. Admittedly, these types of questions are going to be more difficult for the students to know the answers to at the beginning of a lesson.

1) Can you identity five key quotes about Elizabeth Bennett and their importance from this extract?

2) What is your reaction to Elizabeth Bennett as a reader? How do you feel about her as a character? Can you provide evidence from the extract to support your feelings?

3) How do your selected quotations compare to each other? Which one is the most effective and why?

Turning the learning outcomes into questions in this way makes it easier to assess progress. It is much easier to ascertain the quality of a student's answer to a question if outcomes are presented in this way. Students also feel more able to respond to questions and can structure their answers more easily.

Some other learning outcomes that could be used as questions are as follows which will definitely ascertain knowledge and understanding before the lesson starts.

Key Stage 3 – Persuasive writing

1) Can you identify four pieces of persuasive writing that you might encounter in everyday life?

2) What are five key features of persuasive writing?

3) Can you work out what this mnemonic about features of persuasive writing means? F.E.A.R. Can you give an explanation for each of the features?
   F   Facts
   E   Exaggeration and emotive language
   A   Assertions and anecdotes
   R   Rhetorical questions

Asking questions that are essentially learning outcomes in this way helps you as the teacher to ascertain how much knowledge the students have about persuasive writing. Most of the students are going to be able to answer questions one and two but few will be able to answer question three.

If this does prove to be the case then you know that you can focus your lesson on teaching the students about the use of the features of F.E.A.R. and see whether they can recognise them in examples of persuasive writing before including it in their own writing.

Presentation of outcomes as questions requires engagement from the students from the start of the lesson as they are having to assess their own knowledge rather than being told that by the end of the lesson they will know what F.E.A.R. means and be able to include it in their own writing.

Teacher acting as a funnel for question and answer sessions

One of the common mistakes that teachers make when asking questions in a class is to create this kind of scenario:

Teacher: Clare, can you tell me a key point about Mr Birling's character in Act One of *An Inspector Calls*?

Clare: Mr Birling is seen as old fashioned and things like social status are important to him.

Teacher: Thanks Clare, you think that Mr Birling is old fashioned and things like social status are important to him. Well done, that is a good answer.

Unfortunately, if a teacher repeatedly does this within lessons then the rest of the students stop listening to Clare or any other student and only listen to the class teacher as the class teacher repeats all of the students' answers. This can create a passive climate within a classroom as all discussion is funnelled through the teacher and the students start to think that validation of their ideas only occurs when the teacher repeats them. Unfortunately, this approach does not encourage independent thinking, confidence or exchange of ideas to deepen learning.

An alternative could have been:

Teacher: Clare, can you tell me a key point about Mr Birling's character in Act One of *An Inspector Calls*?

Clare: Mr Birling is seen as old fashioned and things like social status are important to him.

Teacher: Thanks, Clare, so Tom, do you agree or disagree with Clare's view?

Tom: Well, yes, he does appear old fashioned as he refers to things that have happened in the past and things like the type of port he serves appear to be important to him.

Teacher: Thank you, Tom. Liz, I am going to give you three minutes to find some quotations on pages 14–16 of the play to support Tom and Clare's view while we carry on with some more questions. Right, James, if Mr Birling appears old fashioned what we do you think about Mrs Birling? In Act One, do we think she is the same or slightly different from her husband?'

This type of questioning does not need hands-up from the students because you as the teacher are directing questions to individuals and you can therefore make your questions easier or harder depending on who you are targeting them at. The inclusion of Liz in finding quotes is also important as learning quotes is central to any English Literature KS4 specification so any dialogue about characters must be supported by evidence from the text. You can then agree or disagree with Liz's selection but by presenting in this way, you are indicating how important evidence is to support ideas.

This type of questioning also 'bounces' the questions around but by asking the students to respond to each other and not to you. This means that they will gain confidence with their opinions and start to engage in the learning from each other and from the actual text.

'Pose, Pause, Pounce, Bounce' question strategy

An extension of this question is the 'Pose, Pause, Pounce, Bounce' strategy that became popular in 2011 when Ross McGill @TeacherToolkit wrote about it in the *Guardian*, www.theguardian.com/teacher-network/2011/nov/17/lessons-good-to-outstanding-afl-questioning.

Essentially, this questioning strategy reinforces how important 'wait' time is before answering a question. There is increasing evidence that posing key questions and then waiting before asking for an answer increases the quality of the answer. Increasing wait time to 3 seconds for closed questions and 10 for open increases the quality of the response. This research into the impact of wait time was conducted initially by Mary Budd Rowe and published in her article titled 'Wait Time: Slowing Down May Be a Way of Speeding Up!'.

Ross McGill explains the outline of how to deliver the Pose, Pause, Pounce, Bounce (PPPB) strategy in his article as referenced above. In an English classroom it could look as follows:

Class studying 'London' by William Blake

Teacher (Pose):   The title of the poem tells us as the reader that the poem is about London but what other clues are there in the poem that it is about London or about a city?

(Teacher Pause – no hands up – count in your head – 1 and 2 and 3 and 4 and 5)

Teacher (Pounce):	Jason, what clue have you found in the poem?
Jason:	I have found that it mentions the river Thames.
Teacher (Bounce):	Thanks, Charlotte, what does Blake say about the Thames?
Charlotte:	Blake says it is 'charter'd'.
Teacher (Pose):	I am going to ask you all to think about what 'charter'd' might mean as Blake mentions it in the first line. What could it mean and what does it tell us about how Blake might feel about London?

(Teacher Pause – no hands up – count in your head – 1 and 2 and 3 and 4 and 5)

Teacher (Pounce):	Joe, what do you think charter'd means in this poem?
Joe:	I think it means laid out like on a map – maybe in a pattern?
Teacher (Bounce):	Thanks, Joe. Right, Elise, now we understand what charter'd means as Joe is correct, what does that word suggest about how Blake might be presenting London to the reader?
Elise:	Blake might be telling us that it is all the same. All the problems are the same as he then says something about 'marks of weakness, marks of woe?' in every face he meets. Is he saying that everyone in London suffers and all are filled with sadness?
Teacher (Bounce):	Thanks, Elise. Charlie, do you agree with Elise's view and does woe mean sadness?

This is an example of PPPB in an English lesson and admittedly it needs you as the teacher to know your students, as you need to know who to 'bounce' the questions to, so that the information that is being shared is generally accurate. Also note that there is no direct validation either of 'well done Charlotte' or 'excellent answer Joe'. By moving on to another student then it is implicit that the answer is correct and worthy of expansion. However, there is a direct reference to confirm that Joe is correct, as it can be difficult to offer no validation for any points that are given to you. However, by not praising each answer, it reduces your contribution to the discussion and allows you to 'bounce' the questions to specific individuals. This lack of validation also means that students build up their confidence about their ideas and ability to share them as a quick smile from you as a non-verbal gesture can provide them with all the feedback that they need in this type of exchange in a classroom.

For these types of questioning sessions, it is worth planning the key questions you want to ask or at least the areas you want to cover, i.e. concept of mapping and how it reinforces the idea of a pattern within the poem 'London'. Unlike the use of lollipop sticks or the random name generator, which are also popular strategies for questioning, this type of use of PPPB allows you to target your question to individuals, which is indicative of their ability or engagement in the lesson.

This type of 'pose' and then 'pause' allows all to be involved in the questioning activity and not to feel like a 'rabbit in the headlights' when their name is pulled out on a lolly stick or generated on a PowerPoint display. There are places for both of those types of questioning strategies but use of the PPPB strategy in this way allows the student to build up their skills as well as their knowledge of the poem. More importantly, it allows you to be in control of the types of questions so that success is felt by all students in the classroom which means that engagement will ultimately increase as a result of this type of activity.

Depth of Knowledge

As an outstanding teacher, you will have heard of Bloom's Taxonomy and how it can be used to generate questions and even learning outcomes (as discussed in Chapter 2).

However, an alternative to Bloom's Taxonomy could be to explore 'depth of knowledge' which was developed by Dr Norman Webb (1997) from the University of Wisconsin. He created these Depth of Knowledge (DOK) levels to help ensure standardisation of assessments across a number of states in America. However, it has grown in recognition and a paper was published in 2009 that links Bloom's Taxonomy and Webb's DOK. The article was written by Karin, K. Hess and colleagues and is called 'What exactly do "fewer, clearer and higher standards" really look like in the classroom? Using a cognitive rigor matrix to analyse curriculum, plan lessons and implement assessments' (Hess *et al.* 2009).

The key difference between the Taxonomy and DOK is that Bloom's Taxonomy describes the 'thinking' process necessary to answer a question. In contrast, the DOK levels relate more closely to the depth of understanding of the content and how the skills are then applied.

The descriptors for Depth of Knowledge are described by Dr Norman Webb as shown in Table 5.1. There are many ways to include these DOK descriptors into questioning strategies and the Edutopia.org website has a range of resources on question stems for DOK and also criteria for assessing reading and writing which could be worth exploring with the demise of levels for KS3, www.edutopia.org/blog/webbs-depth-knowledge-increase-rigor-gerald-aungst.

Table 5.1 Depth of Knowledge levels

DOK	Description
1	**Recall and reproduction** Requires recall of information, such as fact, definition, term, or performance of a simple process or procedure.
2	**Skills and concepts** Use information or conceptual knowledge, two or more steps.
3	**Reasoning and thinking** Requires deep understanding exhibited through planning, using evidence and more demanding cognitive reasoning.
4	**Extending thinking** Requires connections and extensions, high cognitive demands and complex reasoning.

Unlike Bloom's Taxonomy, descriptor 4 is only achievable over time and requires the students to assimilate information and create a response based on their understanding of what they have learned. To use DOK to create tasks that demonstrate conceptual understanding about *Lord of the Flies*, for example, something as listed in Table 5.2 could be created.

Table 5.2 Depth of Knowledge levels in *Lord of the Flies*

DOK	Description
1	**Recall and reproduction** Use a bubble map and write down what you perceive to be examples of civilised and uncivilised behaviour in society. Work out which ones are evident in *Lord of the Flies* from the chapters we have read and locate quotations from Chapters 1–4 that highlight the examples of uncivilised and civilised behaviour in the novel. *National Curriculum KS4 Programmes of Study – seeking evidence in the text to support a point of view, including justifying inferences with evidence.*
2	**Skills and concepts** By using double bubble maps, compare the two types of behaviour, civilised and uncivilised behaviour, that are being exhibited by the boys in Chapters 2–9. *National Curriculum KS4 Programmes of Study – exploring aspects of plot, characterisation, events and settings, the relationships between them and their effects.*
3	**Reasoning and thinking** Joseph Conrad's novel *Heart of Darkness* is a novel about a civilised man's descent into savagery. Write about how Golding presents the 'Heart of Darkness' in *Lord of the Flies* and the conflict that exists between civilised and uncivilised behaviour in the novel. *National Curriculum KS4 Programmes of Study – making critical comparisons, referring to the contexts, themes, characterisation, style and literary quality of texts, and drawing on knowledge and skills from wider reading.*
4	**Extending thinking** *Lord of the Flies* was published in 1954. Golding said about *Lord of the Flies*, 'That really is what the book is about: if you don't have rules, that is to say, if you don't have laws, then you're lost, you're finished, you're gone.' Based on the time of his writing the novel, how do you think *Lord of the Flies* highlights Golding's concerns about society of the current time and the future? *National Curriculum KS4 Programmes of Study – drawing on knowledge of the purpose, audience for and context of the writing, including its social, historical and cultural context and the literary tradition to which it belongs, to inform evaluation.*

I have linked the tasks to the Programmes of Study for KS4 descriptors (July 2014) as outlined in the English National Curriculum so the tasks are not linked to any Assessment Objectives of a specific exam board. www.gov. uk/government/uploads/system/uploads/attachment_data/file/331877/KS4_ English_PoS_FINAL_170714.pdf.

Using Depth of Knowledge levels may offer an alternative to Bloom's Taxonomy for posing questions and tasks as instead it encourages questions/ tasks to be generated to ascertain the depth of knowledge of students by the quality of their outcomes. There is further information about assessment criteria for reading and writing using DOK and also a grid that compares Bloom's Taxonomy and DOK in the article already cited by Hess *et al.* 2009.

Written questions in poetry or other texts

Another strategy is to use written questions especially in the analysis of poetry although it can obviously be used for other texts too. It can add a scaffold and generate an independence for students which ultimately builds up confidence about their skills of analysis.

Analysing texts or poems is a key skill needed for KS3 and KS4 and many students struggle to do this independently; now with unseen poetry as one of the key parts of KS4 exam papers, we have to build up students' independence to achieve this.

Highlight the line or phrases in a poem and then click Insert Comment in a Word document and you will find a text box to type in. You can then insert the questions for the students to work through with as much or as little guidance as you wish (see Figure 5.1). You may have discussed the poem first and introduced the term 'conceit' to the class or not. It also allows you to differentiate the questions as different students can receive different versions of the document with the inserted questions. It takes minimal effort from you as there only needs to be a minor variation of questions for some students but it ensures that are all focused on the task and feel that it is achievable for them.

This type of written questioning strategy allows you to then scaffold the support too because as the students become more skilled at analysis, you can include less in the questions but it ensures that they all feel that they are looking at the 'right' part of the poem and exploring valid ideas.

Quickdraw by Carol Ann Duffy

I wear the two, the mobile and the landline phones,
like guns , slung from the pockets on my hips . I'm all
alone. You ring, quickdraw, your voice a pellet
in my ear, and hear me groan.

You've wounded me.

Next time, you speak after the tone. I twirl the phone,
then squeeze the trigger of my tongue, wide of the mark.
You choose your spot, then blast me

through the heart.

And this is love, high noon, calamity, hard liquor
in the old Last Chance saloon . I show the mobile
to the sheriff; in my boot, another one's

concealed. You text them both at once. I reel.
Down on my knees, I fumble for the phone,
read the silver bullets of your kiss. Take this ...
and this ... and this ... and this ... and this ...

This is a simile – but why do you think the phones are like guns? What does it suggest about what the phones are being used for? Are they being used to hurt each other?

How does this metaphor suggest the Wild West? How does the poet feel about the two phones? Are they in easy reach? Why might this be the case?

What is a pellet? How does the voice sound? Would it be positive or quite negative? Is the voice shouting? How do you know? Whose voice do you think it is?

How does this link to the Wild West? Why does the narrator do this? What does it give the narrator time to do before they say something else?

What does the 'trigger of my tongue' suggest? What has the narrator done? Why are the words that the narrator used so 'wide of the mark' – what impact have the words had on the other person?

How does this link to the Wild West? Is this the make or break stage of the relationship?

What does calamity mean? Why would the relationship ending be a calamity for the narrator?

How does the narrator feel about the relationship at this stage of the poem?

How does the use of the silver bullets help to finish the conceit at the end of the poem? How do you think the poem finishes? With lots of kisses or with lots of angry words?

Figure 5.1 'Quickdraw' from *Rapture* by Carol Ann Duffy.
Published by Picador, 2006. (Source: Copyright © Carol Ann Duffy. Reproduced by permission of the author c/o Rogers, Coleridge & White Ltd., 20 Powls Mews, London W11 1JN)

After the students have worked through these questions, you can ask them to share their ideas within their groups or discuss as a class. However, once again, it will help with ensuring that everyone can contribute to any class discussion as they have all been given the opportunity to achieve and develop their skills of poetry analysis in an independent way.

Answering questions

Another strategy that I have seen when using questions verbally in the classroom is the use of non-verbal gestures to indicate confidence level to give an answer. A stressful incident for a student in the classroom is to be surrounded by a number of students who have their hands up or shout out an answer when they don't know the answer.

An alternative is for students to indicate their knowledge of an answer by simply putting their clenched fist on the desk in front of them and if they don't know the answer then they put their hand spread out on the desk in front of them. This means that teachers can pose a question and instead of waiting for hands-up or targeting individuals they can wait for the sign from a number of students to indicate their confidence in answering a question. It is less of a noticeable physical gesture than hands waving in the air and easier for students to be more honest about their level of confidence or knowledge.

Students generating their own questions

One of the best lessons that I observed was in Science where students were being asked to create an electric circuit by wiring the battery correctly so it turned the light bulb on. The typical method of presenting this type of lesson is to demonstrate to the students how to do it, ask whether there any questions and then ask them to repeat it themselves.

However, in this particular lesson, the students were given all the equipment that they needed to complete the task and were told that they needed to complete the circuit to turn the light bulb on. The students were given approximately six minutes to complete this task and the teacher refused to answer any questions about the task.

After the six minutes, the teacher then brought the class back together and asked what questions they had. There were many, as the students had not been able to complete the task and wanted to know about the specific attributes of the wires and their positioning etc.

This was a class that was generating their own questions as the teacher had given them the outcome first (i.e. the circuit board) and had asked them to work out how to get there. The students were fully engaged as it was a form of problem solving for them which meant they wanted to know the answer.

So, how could this be used in English? I have adapted the same strategy with Shakespeare plays and given students cards of the characters (with pictures of the characters) in *Much Ado About Nothing* with a sentence or two about the characters. I have then asked the students in pairs to link the characters together based on the information that they have and the judgements that they might make about the clothes that the characters are wearing etc.

The students then start asking questions about the characters as they want to know whether their judgements are right. They start using the names of the characters in their dialogue and discussing the attributes of them based on the written and visual information that they have been given.

I have asked them to share their judgements with each other and explain their reasons and also to do a short written prediction activity about what they think will be the plot of the play based on their character predictions. I have taken photographs of their character predictions and as we read the play, I display these photos on the board and we discuss the relevance of their judgements and who was more successful and who was not.

Another similar strategy to generate questions from the students is to give them a type of writing, e.g. persuasive, descriptive or argument, and then ask them to work out what it is and how they know. What are the features they recognise? How effective are they? This is instead of telling them that in that lesson they will be studying descriptive writing and first of all they will be looking at a model of it. The students tend to start asking you as the teacher questions as they want to know whether their opinions and knowledge about descriptive writing are correct.

Finally, another example could be to ask the students to write a diary entry in the style of a soldier in World War I right at the start of a lesson about war poetry. This would normally be your outcome, having studied some war poetry, so the students can use the information gained to write a diary entry. However, by asking the students to do the writing at the start of the lesson, they then start asking questions about what happened in World War I? Why are they doing the task? What does their writing need to include to sound like a diary?

In all these cases, giving the students the 'outcome' or at least some of the outcome at the start of the lesson means they want to know how to be successful at it. It is a more engaging and interactive way of presenting activities to the students if effectively the lesson starts at the end and then works backwards. The amount of questions that you will receive from the students will increase as they will naturally want to know how to be successful at it.

What's in a question?

There is a book called *Teaching Backwards* written by Andy Griffith and Mark Burns (2014) which you might find informative if you are interested in the concept of 'teaching backwards'.

Summary

The aim of questioning is to encourage students to think for themselves about the answers and then have the confidence to share them, verbally or in writing. Some of the aims of the new National Curriculum for English are that students:

1   use discussion in order to learn and should be able to elaborate and explain clearly their understanding and ideas;

2   are competent in the arts of speaking and listening, demonstrating to others and participating in debate.

Use of questions by teachers but also by students between themselves is key for success in achieving these particular aims of the National Curriculum.

Wragg and Brown (2001) in their book *Questioning in the Secondary School* suggest a mnemonic to help with planning questions when planning lessons. They suggest that based on their research the best key questions contain a sense of looking ahead, helping the lesson to move on.

They have created the mnemonic IDEA:

I   Identify the key questions in relation to your outcomes for the lesson.
D   Decide on the level and order (timing) of the questions.
E   Extend the questioning. Think of supplementary and subsidiary questions to ask.
A   Analyse the answers that you are likely to receive and the responses that you might receive.

Key questions to help move learning on need to be planned in advance, as teachers who think 'on the spot' ask questions that are very similar and don't actually stimulate any new learning but are just reinforcing ideas or concepts for students. Therefore, many of these types of questions can be easily accessible for many students in the class and can provide a 'false' impression of progress.

Asking a question that students cannot answer is not a bad thing as long as, during the lesson, you return to the difficult question and ascertain whether students can now answer it. How many can answer it? Who cannot answer it and why? What can you as teacher do to help them be able to answer it? Do you need to do something different or does the student need to do something different to help develop their understanding?

All these points help to underpin the importance of questioning in the classroom and as I said at the start of the chapter, asking the right question in an English lesson which then creates a myriad of responses or ideas from students is one of the highlights in any English teacher's day.

References

Duffy, C. A. (2006) *Rapture*, London: Picador.

Griffith, A. and Burns, M. (2014) *Teaching Backwards*, Wales: Crown House Publishing.

Hess, K. K., Carlock, D., Jones, B. and Walkup, J. R. (2009) What exactly do 'fewer, clearer and higher standards' really look like in the classroom? Using a cognitive rigor matrix to analyse curriculum, plan lessons and implement assessments', Education Resources Information Center (ERIC) publication.

Rowe, M. B. (1986) 'Wait Time: Slowing Down May Be a Way of Speeding Up!' *Journal of Teacher Education*, vol. 37, no. 1, 43–50.

Wragg, E. C. and Brown, G. (2001) *Questioning in the Secondary School*, London: Routledge.

CHAPTER 6

How do I know?

One of the most difficult parts of English teaching is ascertaining how much each student has learnt by a particular stage of the lesson. Inexperienced teachers find that this is the 'holy grail' of teaching as experienced teachers seem to know who is learning in their classroom and they know when and how to assess the learning too.

I don't think there is any 'magic bullet' to explain how assessment can be used in an English classroom as there are too many variables such as size of the class; ability range within the class; topic being studied; nature and type of assessment used within the English department and the list goes on.

This chapter is going to focus on assessment strategies that can be used in the English classroom and how they will help you to work out who has made progress in your lessons and who has not.

At this point, it is probably useful to clarify the various assessment strategies that could be used and their Assessment *for* Learning (AfL), assessment *as* learning and assessment *of* learning.

Assessment *for* Learning is formative assessment. This means that various strategies are put in place in the classroom for students and teachers to engage in a dialogue about the students' knowledge and learning. The information that the teacher receives about the level of learning is meant to affect the subsequent teaching of a future lesson or of the very next activity within a lesson. AfL should provide the teacher with information about what the students have learned and then the teacher should adjust their teaching accordingly. For example, repeat an idea or a concept in a different way as a number of students don't understand it or move on quickly to a new idea as the teacher realises that many of the students have been taught an idea before so already know it. AfL was a key concept introduced by Black and Wiliam (1998) and is an integral part of school improvement.

Assessment *as* learning is when the students are encouraged to assess their own work as part of self or peer assessment to help them become clearer about the requirements to be successful in a particular topic or skill. However, peer and self assessment are strategies that need to be explicitly taught to students so they value it as a form of assessment and understand that taking on the role of the assessor helps them to consolidate their own learning and that of others too.

Assessment *of* learning is summative assessment. This means that the teacher assesses the work and puts a grade or attainment mark on a student's work and gives feedback against clear agreed criteria.

What is assessment?

A key question when making any assessment is 'what do the students know when they leave my lesson that they didn't know when they arrived?' It is a simple question but one that should shape the outcomes, activities and assessments within any lesson.

Subsequently, there are a series of assessment key questions you need to think about when linking assessment and your teaching:

1) What are you going to do to check what level of knowledge the students have when they start the lesson?

2) How are you going to assess the students' knowledge at the start of the lesson? What are you going to do if not many students have the right knowledge? What are you going to do if more of the students than you expected have the right knowledge? How is that going to affect your teaching?

3) What are you going to do during the lesson to find out how many of the students are learning which information? Who is learning it fastest? Why? What are you going to do about the students who are not learning it as fast? How is that going to affect your teaching?

4) How are you going to check that the students have gained new knowledge by the end of the lesson? How you going to check that they have genuinely learned it? What is that information going to tell you about what you need to do in future lessons?

None of these questions are easy to answer and they will change on a daily basis depending on the topic and the outcomes but by answering these questions when planning a lesson then assessment of the students either in a formative or summative manner should become easier.

Some strategies that might help to answer the questions are as follows.

Learning outcomes and success criteria

Learning outcomes are key to ascertaining what the students have learned by the end of the lesson but success criteria help the students to understand how to be successful at achieving the learning outcomes. It avoids the 'guess what is in the teacher's head?' game which can be a problem for students when how to be successful at a task is not explicitly shared with them.

Some possible outcomes when studying a particular poem could be:

Learning outcomes

1) Explain the poetic features of the poem 'Dulce Et Decorum Est' by Wilfred Owen.

2) Assess the impact of the poem's language on the reader.

Success criteria

The success criteria that break down the outcomes could be:

- I can find at least four similes in the poem and explain their meaning.
- I can find an example of alliteration and explain how it adds drama to the description of the gas attack.
- I can find examples of five verbs that help to explain the description of the soldier dying because of the gas attack. I can explain why the choice of these words help me as the reader to feel the drama of the soldier's death.
- I can examine the rhyming pattern of the poem and explain whether or not I feel that the rhyme gives the poem a regular or irregular rhyming structure.
- I can identify the point in the poem when Owen is talking to us as a reader and what the message is that he is trying to convey to his reader about the cruelty of World War I.
- I can determine the meaning of the title of the poem and how we know that Owen was being ironic with his choice of title based on the final lines of the poem.

Learning outcome

- To create a piece of writing to describe a beach or funfair.

Success criteria

- I have used at least ten adjectives in my first two paragraphs.
- I have used sentences that include commas and semi-colons.

- I have used at least five sentences that are only about three or four words long.

- None of my sentences are longer than ten to twelve words.

- I have used at least three paragraphs that are linked using connectives.

- My opening paragraph does not immediately identify that I am describing a beach or a funfair.

- I have only written in the past, present or future tense and not mixed them up.

- I have used the first person or third person throughout my writing and not mixed them up.

- Each paragraph has a key topic and ensures that the reader gains more information about the scene.

Some of the above success criteria are very specific and have a numerical content that could be seen as controversial when asking students to engage in a creative task. However, in my experience, many students, especially boys, find it much easier if there is a clear framework for success, e.g. at least ten adjectives and ten to twelve words in a sentence.

Presenting success criteria in this way also enables you to differentiate the content of the learning outcomes. As, for example, the final point for the success criteria for Owen's poem could be tweaked slightly to encourage a detailed piece of independent writing that demonstrates a student's individual response to the poem.

Student led success criteria

Success criteria can be created by you as a teacher but you may find that once a class has been taught endless poems there is time to allow them to create their own success criteria instead. Student led success criteria allow the students to demonstrate their understanding of the various steps that are required to gain knowledge about a poem. Student led success criteria can be edited by you as the teacher but students will gain an engagement and autonomy by being able to demonstrate their understanding by presenting success criteria to you.

Success criteria also underpin successful peer or self assessment as too often students are asked to write 'two stars and a wish' or something similar about each other's work. However, if they don't have clear criteria to assess it against they tend to write comments such as 'You could have used shorter sentences in your work' or 'Your handwriting is a bit difficult to read'. Asking students to assess their own or others' work against success criteria means that they understand the criteria for assessing and also it adds a value and a relevance to the comments they are making.

How do I know?

Using success criteria in the range of ways that I have outlined will help you to answer one of the key assessment questions, '*What are you going to do during the lesson to find out how many of the students are learning which information?*' Students working through clear and transparent success criteria will provide you with the information about what they are learning.

Colour coding learning outcomes

Learning outcomes can be presented to students in a passive way by simply asking them to copy them down or to simply copy down the learning objective from the board, but for the teacher this provides little information about what the students already know or are planning to learn in a lesson.

In Chapter 2, I briefly mentioned assigning colours to learning outcomes which can be the same as the pack of Post-it notes that you have might have.

However, it is worth mentioning again in the context of the four key assessment questions at the start of the chapter. Asking the students to choose their own learning outcome and linking it to a specific coloured Post-it note will enable you to start to answer the question, '*How are you going to assess the students' knowledge at the start of the lesson?*' It will also help you to start to answer, '*How are you going to check that the students have gained new knowledge by the end of the lesson?*'

By choosing their own learning outcome to complete by the end of the lesson, the students will demonstrate to you what they already know about a topic or how confident they feel about it. For example, returning to the learning outcomes about *Pride and Prejudice* in Chapter 2 (see page 12).

You could display the 'locate' learning outcome to the students in pink; the 'analyse' learning outcome in green; the 'compare' learning outcome to the students in yellow. The students are then asked to choose a Post-it note based on the learning outcome that as a minimum they think they can achieve by the end of the lesson. Please note the word 'minimum' as setting high expectations for students is key to becoming an outstanding English teacher.

1) Your learning outcome is to **locate** five key quotes in this extract about Elizabeth Bennett. **Define** why these five key quotes are important. Think about the way Elizabeth looks, talks and acts with other characters.

2) Your learning outcome is to **analyse** your choice of five key quotes and explain how they have an impact on you as the reader. What do we as a reader feel about Elizabeth Bennett? Do we like her or not? Why do we feel like this? Think about what she says and how she interacts with other characters.

3) Your learning outcome is to **compare** the five key quotes and **evaluate** how they achieve their effects on the reader. Which one is the most effective and why?

The students then stick their Post-it note on their book/desk so you immediately know which learning outcome they have chosen. They can also copy their learning outcome (rather than learning objective) into their exercise book if that is school policy. However, I think it is important not to write anything on the Post-it note at this stage.

In order to answer one of the key assessment questions, '*How are you going to check that the students have genuinely learned new knowledge?*' You can do the following as a plenary; display a key activity/question about each learning outcome on the board and ask the students to write their name on the back of the Post-it note and then answer the question/activity on their Post-it note.

For example, keeping with the learning outcomes as above for *Pride and Prejudice*, the plenary activities could be:

1) Write down in two sentences the typical behaviour Elizabeth presents in the extract. You may wish to start with 'Elizabeth always …'.

2) Do you like Elizabeth Bennett or not? Write your reason in two sentences.

3) Which one of the quotes in the extract is the most effective in explaining the character of Elizabeth? Write down the first few words of the quote and then in two sentences explain why you have chosen it.

At this stage, teachers tend to ask the students to put their Post-it notes in their exercise books or put them on the whiteboard for further discussion. However, you are going to have do something different to that if you are going to be able to answer the key assessment question, '*What is that information going to tell you about what you need to do in future lessons?*'

I would suggest that you have a simple A4 folder with a blank piece of paper in it for each student in your class. Put a student's name on the top of the piece of paper and then collect in the Post-it note from each student and place it on this piece of paper. You could date it if needed. If you continue with this kind of activity then this piece of paper will become filled with more Post-it notes. By keeping a record in this way, you will be able to see whether a particular student is challenging themselves by the colour of the Post-it note, the quality of their answer to the plenary question as well as any misconceptions about the topic too. It is this type of information that gradually builds up information about specific students in your class that will enable you to adjust your teaching and also make personalised interventions for that student in subsequent lessons. This way there is no hiding place for particular students as you can see the progression of their learning over a period of time. I will refer to further uses of the A4 folder later on in this chapter.

Entrance and Exit Tickets

Entrance and Exit Tickets are an extension of the Post-it note idea – by asking students to complete a 'ticket' you are able to ascertain their knowledge at the start and end of the lesson.

Table 6.1 An Entrance Ticket for the start of a Year 7 lesson on nouns

Entrance Ticket	Date:
Name:	Class:
Can you identify all the types of nouns in this list? Write proper, common, concrete, abstract and collective by each of the nouns. swarm happiness Justin Bieber planet aeroplane democracy	

Entrance and Exit Tickets were discussed in Chapter 4 but they are worth mentioning here again as they help you to answer the question, '*What are you going to do to check what knowledge the students have when they start the lesson?*' However, in order to do something with information gained from this ticket, you will need to organise some type of feedback to the answers on the Entrance Ticket so you know which students know the answers and which don't. However, you might have chosen to do what I suggested in Chapter 5 which is ask the students to complete an activity where they are not expected to know the answer. Either way you are going to have to use hands-up or another method to ascertain what knowledge is in the room in order to alter the content of your teaching accordingly.

Table 6.2 An Exit Ticket for the end of a Year 7 lesson on nouns

Exit Ticket	Date:
Name:	Class:
Write a four line description about what you did at the weekend. It must include an example of a proper, common, concrete, abstract and collective noun. Please underline them too.	

This type of activity will help you to answer, '*How are you going to check that the students have gained new knowledge by the end of the lesson?*' However, I think it is only useful to you if it is collected in and put in the A4 folder that I referred to earlier as asking the students to underline the types of nouns in their short piece of writing allows you very quickly to work out who knows what the different types of nouns are and who does not. This collation of information then allows you to alter the content of your teaching in your next lesson if it is apparent that the students are still not able to independently use different types of nouns by the end of the lesson.

If the colour coding of lesson outcomes is one that you wish to explore further, colour coding the Entrance and Exit Ticket to match the outcomes will clearly link the students to the knowledge they have learned. The content of the Entrance and Exit Tickets can be slightly different to match the learning outcome. This type of formative assessment activity will help you to ascertain who has learned what and how well by the end of the lesson.

Quality of interactions with students

Using formative assessment strategies in your lesson to gain information about what the students know is only useful if you then interact with the students and help them to continue to make progress.

The individual intervention by the teacher with students is one of the most important parts of our job and one that perhaps is not explained explicitly enough. John Hattie in *Visible Learning* (2009, pp. 174–178) and other educationalists discuss how the overuse of praise in the form of feedback produces limited results.

For example, 'Well done Joe, you have written lots in that paragraph and I can see you are making progress with the question' is almost pointless in helping Joe to improve. This type of feedback is, according to Hattie, not going to have much direct impact on Joe's progress. Hattie suggests that feedback should be given to students by answering three questions: 'Where am I going?' 'How am I going?' 'Where to next?' (2009, p. 177). He states that 'an ideal learning environment or experience is when both students and teachers seek answers to these questions' (p. 177), and argues that each of the three feedback questions works at four levels: task level, process level, self-regulation level and self level (pp. 176–177).

In an English lesson, a teacher's intervention with a student writing about Benedick's attitude to love and marriage in *Much Ado About Nothing* using Hattie's four levels might look something like:

- Task level – you need to include three more points about the society's feelings about marriage at the time that the play was set.

- Process level – you need to include the five key quotations that we have agreed are important to demonstrate Benedick's attitude to marriage.

- Self-regulation level – you have already shown me in class discussion that you understand that Benedick tries to show us that he does not believe in love and marriage so can you read through your writing so far and check that you have made this clear? Perhaps highlight or underline where you think you have shown this.

- Self level – you have clearly spent time and thought on this piece of writing and now if you include at least four more quotations and demonstrate Benedick's dislike of love and marriage then you will have improved your writing.

The self-level comment tries to draw minimal attention to self as when feedback draws attention to self, e.g. 'Well done' or 'You are a great student', then students try to avoid the risks involved in tackling a challenging assignment, they minimise effort and have a high fear of failure (Hattie, 2009, p. 177).

Hattie says that feedback needs to 'prompt active information processing on the part of the learner, have low task complexity, relate to specific and clear goals and provide little threat to the person at the self level' (2009, p. 117). He adds that 'the art is to provide the right form of feedback at, or just above, the level where the student is working' (p. 177).

Using feedback in the way Hattie describes needs confidence from teachers about what the next level (whatever that might look like in your school) is so that you can move students towards answering 'Where to next?' in any activity that they undertake.

Encouraging reflection time
DIRT – Dedicated, Improvement, Reflection Time

'Dishing the DIRT' is a phrase that is becoming more familiar in classrooms and it describes a strategy where teachers encourage students to engage in a reflective manner with the feedback that they have been given, usually in written work. The term was introduced by Jackie Beere in *The Perfect Ofsted Lesson* (2012), where she explains that it is time given to students to reflect and act upon the targets that have been set.

A rule I always had in my teaching was to come up with strategies that would encourage the students to reflect on their work for as long as it had taken me to mark it. For example, if it had taken me approximately seven minutes to mark a GCSE essay then I would ask the students in various ways to reflect on the comments I had made for about seven minutes. Allowing this amount of time enabled the students to develop their learning to deepen further than 'surface' level and gave them time to improve their work based on the comments that they had received.

A common practice in schools is to issue students with a coloured pen that is different from the teacher's pen so that it is clear to see when the students have reacted to the teacher's comments in their writing.

Another strategy can be to use questions in comments to encourage students to engage with the comments that a teacher has written and for a dialogue to develop.

For example, the following is a comment on a Year 9 'writing to argue' assessment about how a school should spend more money on technology in the classroom for students:

> *Well done Molly, there are clear strengths in your writing. You have included many features of writing an argument such as rhetorical questions; discourse markers and you have started to present two points of views in your writing.*
>
> *However, why did you use the particular anecdote of how boring Maths lessons can be without the use of iPads to support your argument? Do you think you can explain why you decided to use that particular example or can you include one that might be slightly less emotive? Remember, that your examples don't have to be actually true.*

This type of comment starts to encourage a dialogue as Molly might explain why she chose that particular example or she might take the guidance and write another example. Either way if she responds in a different coloured pen then it shows how she has been given the opportunity to improve her writing.

Another way to use coloured pens is to use pink and green pens for summative or formative assessments. Pink pen represents 'tickled pink' which means that the student (if self assessment) or you (if teacher assessment) are happy that the writing demonstrates understanding of the success criteria or learning outcomes. Green pen represents 'green shoots' which means that the student or you as the teacher can indicate where there is some evidence of understanding of the success criteria or learning outcomes but it needs more development or improvement.

As mentioned in Chapter 4, a strategy to encourage reflection is to use the acronym SIR for comments about students' work. At the end of a piece of writing, students can write the following:

S   Strengths at the bottom of their work – leave a few lines

I   Improvements and leave a few lines

R   Reflection.

You as the teacher can write comments in the strengths and improvement sections and then the students once they have read your comments can write their responses or improvements in the reflection space. This type of acronym gives a clear structure to all formal feedback and can help with demonstration of progress.

However, in English I think that any DIRT time needs to be linked to examples of good models of writing. Students can continue to make the same mistakes if DIRT time is not then linked to demonstration of good examples. Teachers need to share high quality models of the writing that they are looking for during the DIRT time so that students can compare and improve their work and understand where they need to go to next.

Marking as a form of assessment

Marking is a burden for many English teachers but planning the learning carefully with the learning outcomes can help ease it slightly.

Here are three strategies that exemplify how important the link is between the learning outcomes and what the students write down in their books and it is the checking of learning that creates the main reasons for marking:

1) The learning outcome is for students 'to apply persuasive features of emotive language; rhetorical questions and anecdotes to their writing'.

    Explain to the students that they will only receive marking in relation to that outcome:
    - 'Yes' means that there is strong evidence that they have included one or all features of the persuasive writing;
    - '?' means that there is not strong evidence;
    - '!" means that that there is little evidence.

    The overall comment at the end of the work can also be brief and say something like 'Well done for the effort that you put into this piece of writing. Please take time to make improvements to your writing as indicated in my marking.'

    This then provides the opportunity for the students to demonstrate their improvement in green/purple coloured pen underneath your comments but with limited feedback from you. However, your marking will have shown you where the lack of understanding is, so during the lesson you give back the books to the students you probably need to model successful persuasive writing so the students can make improvements in line with your suggestions.

2) Another marking strategy is to number the learning outcomes (1–5) and use these numbers throughout the marking. Then your comment only needs to be 'Well done for your effort'.
   - Your strengths: 1 + 4
   - Areas to improve: 2 + 5

   In the lesson that you give back the students' books, display on the board the learning outcomes from the previous lesson with the numbers. Ask the students to match up the numbers to the ones you have put in the comments in their books. Students are then asked to edit or improve their work in accordance with the numbers that correspond to the appropriate learning outcome.

   You are still assessing the learning of the students as you have made the judgements about the progress against the learning outcomes but you are not writing detailed repetitive comments.

3) As mentioned in Chapter 4, a strategy could be to have three coloured boxes in your room green, amber and red. Establish what the colours mean in that particular lesson. They could mean levels of confidence, levels of attainment or levels of effort according to the learning outcomes.

   As the students leave the classroom they place their exercise books in whatever box they think represents either their level of confidence, attainment or effort as agreed.

   Your marking is to look at their work and write 'I agree' or 'What else could you do to change your level of confidence/attainment?'

   At the point of returning the books, you can ask the students to write a reflective comment about why they think you wrote ' I agree' or ask them to answer your question about 'What else could you do …? However, it is important that once again you share the learning outcomes and the meaning of the green, amber and red colours.

   You are still assessing the learning that is taking place in the lesson and receiving feedback about it but the marking from you is limited as it is all linked to planning the learning and the outcomes.

Assessment without levels

There is no easy answer to how to assess without levels as, at the time of writing this book, English departments are creating their own individual assessment systems for KS3; continuing with existing school assessment strategies or returning to old ones such as the APP grids.

How do I know?

There is lots of information and many views from educationalists about how schools should be approaching assessment without levels at KS3 and this book cannot hope to explore all the various approaches.

However, one tried and tested method that I would like to present, whether your English department uses levels or not, is to take photographs of students' work at various stages of the academic year to indicate progress. These photographs can include whatever assessment strategy your school is using but what it will demonstrate is clear progress. Again, I return to the old-fashioned A4 file and suggest that photographs of students' work are printed out and put in this file alongside the Post-it notes and Exit Tickets demonstrating understanding. If you do this then you will probably need to use file dividers with a student's name on each file divider and put the evidence of the progress of the student behind each file divider.

A photograph of Jake's writing at the start of September with your comments and his comments on it; followed by another photo five or six weeks later again with your and his comments on it; then another one five or six weeks later etc. will create a 'photo album' of success. This A4 folder will then become a powerful form of a markbook as it will outline the progress of all the students in your class which can be shown to students, parents and senior staff and with or without levels it will show progress.

An extension of this idea would to be follow Ron Berger's ideas in *An Ethic of Excellence* (2003) where he suggests that students should present their 'excellent' work as a demonstration of the progress that they have made to achieve it. He says that students should aim for excellence and he believes that 'work of excellence is transformational. Once a student sees that he or she is capable of excellence, that student is never quite the same' (2003, p. 8).

According to Berger (2003, p. 19):

> [T]he most important assessment that goes on in a school isn't done to students but goes on inside students. Every student walks around the school with a picture of what is acceptable, what is good enough. Each time he works on something he looks at it and assesses it. Is this good enough? Do I feel comfortable handing this in? Does it meet my standards? Changing assessment at this level should be the most important goal of every school. How do we get inside students' heads and turn up the assessment so that students have higher standards for their behaviour and their work?

Berger goes onto to talk about how they don't use graded assessment in his school in America but how they used a myriad of assessment tools and conversations with students to assess their competency and understanding. He also says that he is a big fan of student portfolios which is essentially a name that could be given to the A4 folder that I have mentioned a few times in this book.

The student portfolio of evidence could easily be collated by the students or you by taking photographs of their 'best' work which is then shared in a public manner, perhaps at the end of a term or even at a parents' evening where the student has the opportunity to discuss what has made them proud about the evidence in their student portfolio.

Something to think about in the current climate of life in schools without levels in English?

Summary

What do the students know at the end of the lesson that they did not know when they started the lesson?

This is the key question that underpins all the assessment strategies that are outlined in this chapter. Various techniques such as low-stake quizzes, Entrance Tickets, choice of learning outcomes, use of mini-whiteboards and other AfL strategies need to be used at the start of a lesson in order to work out what knowledge the students have or have not retained from one English lesson to the next. A lot of 'life' has taken place between one English lesson and another for a teenager and there can be no expectation that they have retained the knowledge that you had expected them to from one lesson to the other.

Therefore, assessment of current knowledge needs to be made at the start of the lesson in order to correctly ascertain that new knowledge or skills have been learned by the end of the lesson. Increasing research on cognitive science and how students learn suggests that teachers should encourage students to engage in tasks that will allow them to reliably monitor their own learning (*The Science of Learning* by Deans for Impact, 2015). Related to this chapter would be strategies such as Entrance and Exit Tickets, Post-it notes and choice of learning outcomes as well as other strategies discussed in Chapters 4 and 5.

Demonstration of progress in learning and new knowledge can then be demonstrated by using various formative assessment strategies at the end of the lesson as it can be compared to what information was gained about the knowledge of the students at the start of the lesson.

What do the students now know or what can they do at the end of the lesson that they couldn't do at the start? If you can answer that question with some kind of evidence, then you have 'cracked' the assessment of progress and the learning of students.

References

Beere, J. (2012) *The Perfect Ofsted Lesson*, Carmarthen: Crown House Publishing.

Berger, R. (2003) *An Ethic of Excellence*, Portsmouth: Heinemann.

Black, P. and Wiliam, D. (1998) *Inside the Black Box: Raising Standards Through Classroom Assessment*, Phi Delta Kappa International. http://www.pdkintl.org/kappan/kbla9810.htm

Deans for Impact (2015) *The Science of Learning*. Austin, TX: Deans for Impact. www.deansforimpact.org/pdfs/The_Science_of_Learning.pdf

Hattie, J. (2009) *Visible Learning*, London: Routledge.

CHAPTER 7

Thirty different minds in the classroom

Differentiation is about making sure that thirty students make progress in your lesson. 'Personalising learning' is another term that is used interchangeably with 'differentiation'. The term 'personalising learning' indicates that learning should be personalised for all students by using a range of teaching and learning methods. Ensuring that all students make progress in a lesson can be difficult. Therefore, planning is key. You need to ensure in your planning that tasks or activities are personalised to specific groups of students rather than many individual students.

For example, do certain students need specific key words with their meanings given to them at a certain point in the lesson? Placing key terms or tasks on a table directly in front of the students will definitely help particular students who struggle with copying information from the board. Do some students need a very clear writing outline given to them? Do other students need models of how to incorporate analytical and evaluative phrases into their writing? These are all examples of how personalising learning or differentiation can be included in a lesson. These types of resources don't take much time to create as you may have them as part of your lesson but you need to ensure that you give them out to specific students at the right stage of the lesson so that they can refer to them throughout the lesson when needed.

However, differentiation in English is easier than in some subjects. For example, there is not always a 'right' answer to the questions that are asked in an English lesson. In an English classroom we are encouraging differing points of view and as long as the viewpoint is based on some kind of evidence then there is not a 'wrong' answer. For example, you can ask the question, 'How well do you think this writer establishes a relationship with you as the reader?' The answers that you might receive back could range from 'The writer doesn't establish a good relationship with the reader as this novel is boring' to 'The writer does establish a good relationship with the reader as she uses emotive verbs that help us connect with the main character in the novel'. Both of these answers can be considered valid as long as they are supported by reference to the text and this is how a discussion can take place.

As an English teacher, your immediate reaction to the comment, 'This novel is boring' is then to ask, 'Can you give me two reasons why you think this text is boring?' You have not started your point with 'No' or 'Yes' but you are asking the student to explain her answer just like you would ask the other student to give examples of the 'emotive verbs'. Simply, you are asking the students to base their opinions on evidence and not just have an emotive response. You are helping them to develop analytical reasoning which is a life skill that will be used outside education and in the workplace. In an English lesson, we are trying to create an environment where discussion and justification of an individual viewpoint is valued and recognised which does make it easier to differentiate learning.

Ascertaining existing knowledge is a key part of any successful lesson and in order to successfully differentiate you need to know which students have what knowledge and understanding. There are a range of assessment techniques that can be used at the start of a lesson to check existing knowledge. I have outlined many of these strategies in Chapter 4 but it is important to understand that these assessment strategies are giving you information about the students and you have to be prepared to act instantly on the information that they give you. You have to use this knowledge to work out what kind of teaching method you are going to implement in a lesson. This is where you need to have at least three or four teaching methods that you can draw upon to improve the quality of the differentiation in your classroom at any one time. For example, if you are going to teach the use of verbs to a Year 7 class then due to the focus on literacy in primary schools, there is a strong likelihood that many of the students will already know about the use of verbs. Once you have ascertained what they know about verbs at the start of the lesson then you need to be confident that you can adapt your teaching to their needs. Therefore, if you have used differentiated learning outcomes then it is likely one or two of them will still be appropriate for the rest of the lesson. If you have already planned some key questions to ask certain students then you can continue to ascertain their knowledge about verbs. If you have planned differentiated tasks for the students to complete during the lesson then you will have at least one if not two that will still be 'challenging' for the class. By planning differentiation via questioning, tasks and outcomes, you can always ensure that whatever information you gain at the start of the lesson you have enough flexibility to be able to ensure that all students are challenged and develop new learning during the course of a lesson.

Some examples of how to do this are explained more fully in the following section.

Differentiation by questioning

Key questions for a certain part of a lesson can be planned in advance and differentiation can be made clear at this stage of the lesson. Using Bloom's Taxonomy to generate question stems for the various levels of understanding can be very helpful.

The resource Bloom Buster www.tes.co.uk/teaching-resource/The-Bloom-Buster-Improve-Questioning-in-Lessons-6017889/ by Mike Gershon helps to break down each level of Bloom's Taxonomy (it is based on the old version) with appropriate verbs that can be used to generate questions. The lowest level of cognitive thinking is defined as knowledge (remembering) and the highest level of cognitive thinking is defined as evaluation (creating). Using a resource such as Mike Gershon's Bloom Buster allows questions to be planned in advance and aimed at specific students who either represent a specific level of ability or need to be challenged.

For example, teaching the poem 'Ode to Autumn' by John Keats. The types of questions that could be planned and asked within a lesson using the Bloom Buster are as follows:

Knowledge – how does this poem make you feel? Do you like autumn more or less by the end of the poem? Identify specific words from the poem that make you feel either more positive or more negative about autumn.

By asking knowledge questions you are requesting an immediate reaction to the poem but based on evidence from the poem. The next type of thinking you want to encourage is one of understanding.

Comprehension – can you summarise the meaning of each stanza by working out how Keats feels about autumn in each stanza? Does he only pick out the positive features of autumn or does he mention anything negative about autumn in each stanza?

By asking comprehension questions you are ascertaining the students' understanding of the poem by asking them to put in their own words the meaning of each stanza. The next level of thinking is to encourage application. *Can the students apply any previous knowledge to their analysis of the poem?*

Application – can you apply any of the poetic techniques that you have already learned to an analysis of this poem? Can you identify four or five different poetic techniques that Keats uses? After each quotation, can you write down what impact you think this technique has on the reader?

By asking application questions you are encouraging the students to apply their existing knowledge within the context of this poem. Some students may need guidance about what poetic techniques exist in this poem but in all cases you are asking them to work out why the poetic technique has been used by Keats.

*   The next level of thinking is to ask the students to analyse the poem in greater detail, making specific reference to key parts of the poem.*

Analyse – can you decide who the poet is talking to? How do you know? Identify the poetic technique that is being used here and why it is successful. What rhyme scheme is used? Why do you think Keats used it? Does it support the meaning of the poem or not? Why didn't he write it using free verse?

By asking analyse questions you are enabling the student to think carefully about certain features of the poem. They are analysing a specific poetic technique and rhyme scheme by answering these questions. The last question, why didn't Keats write it using free verse is leading them towards the highest more abstract level of thinking which is evaluation. There is no right answer to that question, it is whether they can think of a reason why Keats wrote it as an ode rather than in free verse.

Evaluation – an ode is a style of poem that pays homage or celebrates something. How effectively do you think this poem pays homage to autumn? Does it celebrate the features of autumn enough? Does it celebrate autumn effectively despite using quite a restrictive rhyming structure? Do you think the use of the poetic techniques help the poem to become more visual? Does the use of emotive adjectives generate a positive reaction to this poem?

By asking evaluation questions you are guiding the students to present a clear opinion of the poem but just not an emotive one. You are asking them to look at the positive and negatives sides of the poem. Do they think the poem celebrates autumn and what makes them think that?

These types of questions require some thinking time so they would not be ideal at the start of the lesson when the students have no knowledge of the poem. Ask the students to discuss the questions in pairs for a short time. This will give them peer support and improve the quality of the answers that you will receive. It avoids hands-up as everyone has had time to think about the questions and it allows you as the teacher to target your questioning to certain students (plan in advance which students will be answering the questions) as you wish to check their understanding due to their ability or because you wish to challenge them. Using Bloom's Taxonomy in this way ensures that you are structuring the students' thinking in a clear differentiated way that enables them all to access the higher as well as the lower order thinking skills.

Differentiation by task

Differentiation by task is often done by asking certain students depending on their ability to do either more of a task or less of it. However, this is not always a successful approach as developing new learning is not achieved by this strategy.

A strategy to try is to colour code tasks when they are presented to the students. You can either put a level (or whatever system your school is using) or the tasks can be presented with various colours assigned to them. I would suggest that the colours are not significant, e.g. try to avoid the RAG (red amber green) colouring as the students will assume that the green colour is the easy task. I have seen some teachers assign characters or images that are appropriate to the context of the lesson to the various tasks.

Paul Ginnis in his document 'Learning Principles & Planning Prompts' (2010) discusses how the use of verbs can double up as assessment criteria. He states that these verbs 'automatically suggest the behaviours, tasks or activities that will assess the extent to which the learning has been internalized by the students' (p. 4).

The top verbs in Figure 7.1 are encouraging surface thinking whereas the lower ones are encouraging deeper thinking:

1. reproduce, recall, list, recite, state, quote, imitate, repeat, locate, identify, label, describe
2. define, summarise, outline, reword, paraphrase, calculate
3. explain, convey, demonstrate, present, teach, model
4. apply, interpret, adapt, utilise, solve, manipulate, employ, rework, convert, relate, transpose, translate, implement
5. dissect, examine, reason, argue, analyse, investigate, sort, categorise, deconstruct, convince, scrutinise
6. compare, combine, blend, develop, re-organise, join, structure, integrate, contrast, classify
7. assess, evaluate, judge, conclude, weigh, rate, rank, appraise, arbitrate, determine
8. create, invent, originate, generate, fashion

Figure 7.1 List of assessable verbs from Ginnis (2010)

Therefore, if setting a writing task about 'Ode to Autumn' by John Keats the tasks could look something like this:

1) How does this poem appeal to the reader's senses? Find and write down at least five examples from the poem about how Keats engages the reader's different senses. You need to pick out key words from each of your examples and explain how they relate to one of our human senses.

2) Do you think that Keats liked the season of autumn? Examine the poem and find at least four examples of where you think Keats shows whether he likes or dislikes the season. Within each quotation that you select, you need to examine the language and identify poetic techniques and emotive language that Keats uses to demonstrate his feeling towards autumn.

3) Do you think that 'Ode to Autumn' is an effective poem? Assess the poem and discuss whether you think its use of poetic techniques, rhyming structure and content help the reader to either like or dislike autumn. You need to find at least six quotations and examine them in detail for various techniques used by the poet.

These tasks could be presented to the students with various colours associated to them. For example, match the outcomes to the Post-it notes that you just have every day in your classroom. I suggest that you mix them up so it is not obvious that no. 1 is always the easiest one but I have kept them in this order so you could see how it is linked to Paul Ginnis' verbs. However, I would suggest that you always mix up the order and the colours/symbols for different lessons so the students are not easily able to 'pigeon hole' themselves.

For example – highlight the wording of Task 1 in orange and ask the students to take an orange Post-it note to indicate which task they are doing; blue for Task 2 and pink for Task 3. You could then ask them to write on their Post-it note a sentence about how well they feel they achieved their task by the end of the lesson and ask them to hand these in or share them with you. Alternatively, you can print out these tasks on different coloured paper and the students come up to the front and choose which task they are doing.

Having the colours or the symbols attached to each task gives you a visual sign about which tasks the students are doing. You can then intervene as appropriate. If a student has chosen a task that is too easy, you can then challenge them to do the harder one. If a student has chosen tasks that you think might be a little too difficult you can encourage them by acknowledging that you appreciate that they are challenging themselves. By not using the levels and using colours or symbols instead, you are giving the students a choice and allowing them to take charge of their own learning journey for that lesson. We all know that once an element of choice is involved in anything then our level of engagement is raised. Supermarkets, for example, have the concept of choice and engagement very clearly linked together as they know it is an extremely successful combination.

Differentiation by learning outcomes

The concept for differentiation by learning outcomes is similar to the one for tasks. The use of Paul Ginnis' learning verbs can also help with writing differentiated learning outcomes. Schools use a range of methods to present learning outcomes – WALT/WILF – Some, Most, All – Level 4, Level 5 and Level 6 etc.

However, defining differentiated learning outcomes is not always easy as too often learning outcomes become what the students are 'doing' rather than what they are 'learning'. Too often I have sat in lesson observations and heard a colleague who is observing with me say 'the students are doing really well – they seem really engaged with the activity.' However, the question to then ask is 'what are the students actually learning?' They may be 'doing really well' but what are they learning that is new? Are they just 'doing' something that they already know and that is why they look engaged?

Learning objectives are the general overview of the lesson – 'to learn/understand the language that Keats uses in "Ode to Autumn" and the impact that it has on the reader' is a general learning outcome. It gives an idea of the topic of the lesson but it does not define specifically the assessable learning.

Therefore, differentiated learning outcomes to support this objective and to demonstrate progress would be:

1) Define the poetic techniques that Keats uses and whether he shows the reader that he likes autumn.

2) Examine the language and the poetic techniques that Keats uses and discuss the impact that these have on the reader.

3) Evaluate the effectiveness of the poem 'Ode to Autumn' and its impact on the reader.

These are differentiated learning outcomes using Paul Ginnis' assessable verbs to determine whether a student has been able to 'define' the poetic techniques. You can see whether students have started to use analysis in their writing when they have shown an 'examination' of the poem. You can also see whether students have 'evaluated' the poem when they have outlined what the poet has done well (with evidence from the poem) and what could be better (with evidence from the poem). This is a high order skill.

These learning outcomes can be presented to the students (again in a mixed up order) and they could individually write down which learning outcome they are going to achieve by the end of the lesson instead of simply copying down the learning objective which is a 'bell work' strategy that is used by many schools. Again, this is encouraging the students to make a choice and take responsibility for their learning in the lesson.

The learning outcomes can be presented using visual images too. For example, when I taught *Pride and Prejudice* to Year 10 students I presented them with the lesson's outcomes which were connected with images of the book. For copyright reasons, the images cannot be included but I have included in each text box links to the various film posters for *Pride and Prejudice* which in itself will create a discussion about various interpretations of the book.

Your learning outcome is to locate five key quotes in this extract. Define why these key quotes are important in this extract.

www.teachwithmovies.org/guides/pride-and-prejudice-files/DVD-cover-2005.jpg

---

Your learning outcome is to analyse the five key quotes and determine why they are important in this extract with regards to plot and character development.

http://modernmrsdarcy.com/wp-content/uploads/2011/08/Darcy-and-Elizabeth-e1313521962809.jpg

---

Your learning outcome is to evaluate your choice of five key quotes and explain how they have an impact on you as the reader.

http://livelikeyouarerich.com/wp-content/uploads/2014/05/pride-and-pred.jpg

---

The use of visual images acted as a way of reminding the students that there are different interpretations of *Pride and Prejudice*. It also allowed me to have a discussion about the learning outcomes with individual students without the labels of levels but with images that were relevant to their learning.

Additionally, these learning outcomes showed a learning journey for that lesson as if the students started with the first one 'locate five key quotes' then they could move into the second one 'analyse key quotes' and finally 'evaluate the key quotes'. Presenting the learning outcomes in this way made sure that all the students could see how the learning journey fitted together and encouraged them to start at a suitable place for them and then move onwards. It made the differentiation explicit to them but at the same time encouraged them to challenge themselves as it clearly showed all of them what they were aiming to do; i.e. the 'brilliant outcome' is to be able to 'evaluate the quotes and explain which is the most effective and why'.

Challenge/extension task

Another way of differentiating by task is to have a challenge or extension task planned for those students who you think need it. A successful way of doing this is to put it in an envelope either on the students' tables or kept at your desk and they have to ask you for it. The students like the intrigue of opening the envelope especially if it is labelled with CHALLENGE on the front. They like the status that it gives them in front of their peers and it avoids giving them the label of being too keen by asking for more work. Using coloured envelopes seems to work well and they are very resusable.

Differentiation with students with specific learning needs

The SEND Code of Practice 2014 outlines the key obligations that schools and other organisations have to people who are defined as having special needs or disabilities, www.gov.uk/government/publications/send-code-of-practice-0-to-25

Working with students with specific learning needs can be one of the most challenging aspects of teaching, especially if you don't have a teaching assistant on a regular basis in your classroom.

Students who have autism will be on a continuum of autistic behaviours and each individual student will display a specific range of behaviours. Therefore, think about your non-verbal language when working with autistic students. Be aware that some students don't like to be touched or be in close proximity to you or other students. Think about where they should be seated in your classroom. Think about the routines of your lesson each day and try to ensure that the start of the lesson follows a predictable pattern. For example, students line up outside the door and then enter the classroom to their assigned seat and get out their exercise books etc.

Be aware that many autistic students will not understand inference, they will interpret ideas and instructions literally. For example, if you say to an autistic student, 'Are you hot?' their answer is likely to be either 'yes' or 'no'. They will not infer from the question that you are suggesting that they might wish to take off their school jumper or even that they look hot. You need to therefore think about the sort of questions that you will ask autistic students in front of the whole class. Another feature of autism can be a lack of eye contact. Autistic students may not like making direct eye contact and you must not see it as a lack of concentration.

The National Autistic Society has guidance on working with autistic students in the classroom: www.autism.org.uk/professionals/teachers/in-your-school.aspx.

Students who have dyspraxia will struggle with organisation and also writing down words and phrases quickly. A key way of helping students with dyspraxia is to give them printed material so that they don't have to spend too much time copying and writing down things from the board. Homework should be printed out and or written out for them so it can be put into their planner with a clear date of submission. When asking students with dyspraxia to complete a piece of writing they may find it helpful if you put a mark by the line in the exercise book that you wish them to write to as a blank page could be rather overwhelming. Your knowledge of the student will tell you whether you need to give them praise at various points of the lesson.

The Dyspraxia Foundation has suggestions for working with students with dyspraxia and they have created specific guidance for secondary schools: www.dyspraxiafoundation.org.uk/wp-content/uploads/2013/10/Secondary_Classroom_Strategies.pdf.

Students with dyslexia will have barriers to working with the written word for various reasons and you need to develop their confidence in your classroom. You can encourage dyslexic students to present their ideas in a variety of ways, e.g. diagrams, voice recording, videoing and annotating still photographs. All can be easily done using iPads, mobile phones, flip cameras or other audio devices. You could also introduce dyslexic students to mind mapping (not brainstorming), where ideas are coherently generated using colours and other codes.

Take a look at Tony Buzan's website http://thinkbuzan.com for an understanding of mind mapping. There is now a range of mind mapping software packages that can be bought too. Another strategy is to use a 'buddy' system within your class, a nominated student who the dyslexic student works with and can check with if they are struggling to interpret information or tasks. Don't leave homework or other big tasks to the end of the lesson. If you have to do this then I would suggest that you print off the homework task or other significant tasks and give it out to the dyslexic student as copying down writing under pressure is something that some dyslexic students will struggle with. Ensure that there are lots of speaking and listening tasks incorporated within the lesson so these can be shared within groups or with the 'buddy' student as the dyslexic student will gain confidence from knowing that their verbalised ideas have value. You will also need to decide on marking strategies when assessing dyslexic students' work. You need to agree on certain targets with them and then focus on these in your marking, as having pen marks all through their writing will be very dispiriting.

The British Dyslexic Association has a very useful website that can be accessed from this link – www.bdadyslexia.org.uk/files/dfs_pack_English.pdf

Support notes

These are notes that can be given to specific students once a task has been set for the whole class and they have started working. For example, you can give support notes with line and page numbers to specific students who struggle to read long passages if the task is to answer some comprehension questions on a specific chapter.

You could give out a glossary of poetic terms to certain students, e.g. personification and onomatopoeia if studying 'Ode to Autumn', to help them identify key techniques in a poem. These can be given out discreetly once the whole class is working on the task and you can hand them out to the specific students with the phrase 'just in case you need it'. Obviously, it doesn't need to be titled 'Support notes' – that is just the term that I have used here.

Visual images

Visual images work very well with students who have English as an Additional Language. Downloading some pictures from the internet that are connected with the topic of the lesson or drawing them yourself with the English words underneath with space for the student to write the same words in their own language is a very successful strategy. The use of cartoon strips for certain novels and poems can be very useful to track the ideas of linear plots. The next stage is then to encourage the students to create a glossary of the words that they are using with these visual images so that they have the English words with their own language words next to each other. If you provide them with an exercise book to do this in then they can take it with them to other lessons and gradually transfer this strategy into their other subject lessons which will help them develop their English vocabulary.

Working with teaching assistants

Ask most teaching assistants and they will tell you that they are an underused resource mainly because teachers and teaching assistants do not have time to communicate with each other on a regular basis. This is definitely the case if you only see each other once a week.

Creating a document that gives a short overview of the lesson and what you want the teaching assistant to do which you can hand them as they enter the classroom is an invaluable resource. It does not take very long to create, something similar to Table 7.1, and it can be reused and adapted for many lessons. The key point of this type of document is that you as the teacher are clearly identifying what you want the nominated students to learn in the lesson and then you are asking for the teaching assistant's comments. This encourages a cohesion of the learning into the next lesson even if the teaching assistant is not present. It also allows you to keep an ongoing record of the progress and learning that specific students are achieving throughout a unit of work.

Table 7.1 Working with learning support assistants in English lessons

Date of Lesson: 9 February 2014 – Period 3	
Students I would like you to work with today are:	William Chloe
Learning outcomes of today's lesson for William and Chloe are:	Locate four key quotations in the poem 'Ode to Autumn'. Copy them down and underline any words that identify whether the poet likes the season of autumn or not.
Resources we are using today:	Copies of 'Ode to Autumn', exercise books and my PowerPoint for today's lesson (attached)
The skills I would like you to develop with them are:	William – use of full stops and commas Chloe – spelling of poetic terms
The knowledge that I would like you to check that they have is:	Do both of them understand the meaning of 'Ode to Autumn'? Do they know what it is about and can they find the key quotations and highlight the key words that identify the poet's feelings about autumn?
Your comments – what did William and Chloe learn today and what do you think we need to have in place for next lesson for them?	
Teaching assistant – sign and date:	

Summary

Differentiation is key for ensuring that all learners make progress. For example, students with a specific learning need or students who are of a high ability should all be able to make significant progress in an English lesson.

Some key points to remember are:

- Check what knowledge is in the room at the start of the lesson. (Strategies to do this are given in an earlier part of the book.) What do your students know already?

- Plan questions in advance for specific parts of your lesson and target these questions to certain students who represent an ability range within your classroom. During the course of three one hour lessons, you should have asked every student to be involved in questioning activities. It can be answering a pre-planned question or you can ask them to respond to another student's comments. Being involved with questioning activities should not include an answer to a recall or simple knowledge question. Use Bloom's Taxonomy to help you plan some of these 'hinge' questions in advance.

- Use differentiated learning outcomes and tasks to encourage students to make their own choices. You can use Paul Ginnis' assessable verbs to help you do this.

- Use visual images, challenges and support notes to help nurture students in various ways and ensure that they can all access their learning.

- Make better use of any teaching assistants that are in your classrooms. Create a document that you can both use to outline and then check the learning of specific students in your lessons.

Reference

Ginnis, P. (2010) 'Learning Principles & Planning Prompts: To help you re-design lessons, schemes of work and curriculum'. http://s290088243.websitehome.co.uk/ginnis/images/stories/ginnis/downloads/Learning%20Principles%20&%20Prompts.pdf

CHAPTER 8

The classroom environment

This chapter will discuss the issues of creating a positive physical and emotional classroom environment to aid the learning and progress of students.

Classroom displays

Displays in classrooms can be used as a teaching tool for students in which key questions are asked and students are asked to interact with them. This might be ideas such as a progress wall (students move their name up a ladder identifying their progress in skills or knowledge) or placing Post-it notes on a display in answer to key questions. Again, photographs of student answers can be taken on a regular basis and added to the class display to indicate overall class progress.

When using displays in a more traditional manner to show students' work, Ron Berger in *An Ethic of Excellence* (2003) suggests that the type of student work that is displayed should only be the best that a student can create. There is more you can read in his book about how presentations of students' work can be delivered to an audience at the end of a year or a term which summarises their journey of drafting, redrafting to creating pieces of excellent work that demonstrate their level of understanding and competency.

Putting posters up around a classroom or key phrases that students must engage with during a lesson can be a popular interactive method too. For example, an A3 poster with the word 'Nouns' on the top of it, or 'Verbs'. These are displayed around a room and students with Post-it notes (student initials on the top) are asked to write down a noun or verb that they know. All students use one colour Post-it note for this activity. As the plenary of the lesson, all students are asked to visit each poster and put down an example of a more complex type noun or verb that they have learned about within the lesson in a different coloured Post-it note, again with student initials in the corner. You can then take a photograph of these posters at the end of the lesson and refer to them at the start of the next lesson to demonstrate the learning that took place during one lesson and how as a class they are now going to build on that pace of learning. This demonstrates setting high expectations but also progress in lessons as again these types of photos can form part of your 'student portfolio' for each class, which I have discussed in Chapter 6.

A 'washing line' is also a type of display that is quite common in English classrooms as it allows key words and definitions of terms such as alliteration, personification, enjambment to be displayed across the middle of the room as each piece of paper is clipped to the 'washing line'.

An alternative could be to use quick response (QR) codes on wall displays in order to encourage students to visit websites from their mobile phones or other devices that are relevant to a text that they might be studying. There are many websites that will generate QR codes for you free of charge if you provide the URL address. This builds on the concept of using displays to add curiosity for students as a tool to encourage them to learn more about a text or a poem that is being displayed. Advertising uses this technique all the time, explaining a key idea or concept on an advert but using the QR codes displayed on the adverts for customers to learn more about their product. Using electronic devices to gain information is a key part of every teenager's life and there is an argument that educational displays in schools should start to engage in that process too even if the QR code takes them to the English Department's revision section on the school website.

Student contribution in lessons

The contribution of students in lessons as we all know can depend on the time of day it is, day of the week and whether it is snowing or raining outside. There are some ways to use technology to help you increase the number of student interactions in your lessons that will help to create the positive and supportive culture needed in a classroom.

Many teachers are probably familiar with the programmes that can create random class name generators and there are some free resources to help you create these.

The random name generator ensures that all students feel a level of commitment and accountability within a lesson as they know that any of them can be asked to answer a question.

Another technique is to use voting pads to obtain information and feedback about students' knowledge and understanding. Promethean, one of the key producers of whiteboards, has voting pads that are compatible with their whiteboards. They are called student response devices and the best thing about them is they will record and collate the student responses for you so you can create spreadsheets and other documents with information about student progress www.prometheanworld.com/en-gb/products/student-response-devices/activote. It requires a little 'set up' time with the registration of the devices within a class but once that is done it is quicker each time they are used. SMARTboards also have the facility too and this is through an enabled mobile device such as a student mobile phone or iPad.

A cheaper way of obtaining student feedback and interaction is to use QR codes. A website www.plickers.com allows you to download an app on your mobile phone; the students hold up printed out QR codes and you can interpret the information that they provide as cards can be assigned to specific students but they can also be used across different classes too, so you can reuse them. It allows the students to answer the questions without everyone else knowing what their answers are, again, helping to build up a supportive environment.

All of these strategies help to create an environment in a classroom that has a 'healthy tension' as students know that they all have to contribute in a non-threatening manner but they are all accountable for engagement within the lesson. It helps to move away from relying on 'hands-up' where inevitably certain students will always be asked to answer questions and other students will be asked to answer questions less often.

Group work

Group work is a strategy that many teachers use to create a cooperative and positive learning environment. However, as an outstanding teacher it is essential to create group work strategies that ensure all students are accountable for the outcomes. Groups can look like they are working together while a teacher is in close proximity but as the teacher moves to help another group, the discussion can turn to chat about weekend plans or the latest contestant to leave *Big Brother*.

At the end of time allotted for a group discussion, teachers invariably say, 'Who can now share your ideas about the key events in Chapter 2?' A student within the group puts up their hand and the teacher can be led to believe that the learning that this particular student is articulating is the same for all members of the group. However, if you ask a colleague to observe the interactions of group discussions within one of your lessons, you will be surprised at how much of the discussion is not about learning and how it tends to involve only one or two students. So how can you improve this?

The classroom environment

1) Students are asked to pass round a piece of sugar paper (or A3 paper) on which they all write their ideas down. For example, how many poetic techniques can you find in this poem? One piece of sugar paper can be passed around the table and each student has to write one poetic technique on it. This means that when you ask for student feedback, you can point to a technique and ask, 'Who wrote this?' You can then ask for that student to share their point. Another extension of this is to give each student a different coloured pen on each table so you know who has written what.

2) You can build on this strategy by circulating four pieces of paper around each group of four by asking the students to write down one idea each time that has not already been written down. For example, write down one or two words that you would use to describe Lady Macbeth, Macbeth, Macduff and Banquo. Each of these four pieces of paper are circulated around each group for a specific number of times and you can easily see which students are contributing and who is struggling. You can also see the quality of their answers and intervene as appropriate. Students know they have accountability for the outcome of the task and that any of them can be asked to share their ideas as you can link the point to a particular student.

3) A further development to encourage student accountability is to assign numbers or coloured Post-it notes to students. You can assign students a specific number in a group, a coloured counter/button or a coloured Post-it note. After a period of discussion, when you ask questions to a group or ask for their views, you can say, 'I would like to hear from students who are number 3' or 'students with green Post-it notes' etc. Again, this means that all students are accountable for the quality of the learning within the group as they know that any one of them can be asked to contribute. This means that student engagement is inevitably raised as they will clarify points with each other and ask questions to ensure that they are able to make a comment to the whole class if they are asked. Another way to mix that up slightly is after hearing from three groups with 'student number 3' you can then say, 'I would now like to hear from number 1' in each group. This means that a whole class can never become complacent when groups are feeding back ideas to you as the teacher.

Seating plans

Seating plans tend to be used to help with behaviour for learning and at the start of a new year and with unknown classes; a standard boy/girl seating plan is implemented to help with behaviour and to also let the class know that you as the teacher are the person who controls the seating in the lesson. It proves to be a very effective strategy for any first lesson with an unknown class and then 'tweaks' can be made as you gain knowledge about the students.

However, seating plans can be used for different purposes too. In English, quite a successful one is to have seating plans called learning partners and progress partners. Each seating plan can have an image or icon associated with it which is relevant to the topics you are studying, e.g. learning partners could be Scrooge and progress partners could be Marley if studying *A Christmas Carol* or you can make it something humorous and personal to a class.

Learning partners is the seating plan where a discussion based lesson is going to take place and progress partners is for a more writing or reading based lesson. The icons for each seating plan can be displayed on the board and once the students know where they sit for each plan, they will quickly seat themselves in the right places as they enter the room. Once the students get used to the concept of various seating plans, it is also possible to change from the progress to the learning partners seating plan within a lesson. It can also allow you to create seating plans that might involve friendship groups and ones that don't. For example, the learning partners one could be derived from friendship groups and progress partners could be structured around the traditional boy/girl seating plan. If students think that there is an option and they don't have to stay in one seating plan all the time then it can help with compliance to the assigned seating plan too.

Positive learning environment

Dealing with a difficult class can be one of the most draining aspects of teaching and as an outstanding teacher you will have tried a range of strategies to help with addressing low level behaviour.

However, one strategy that might help to move the learning relationship forward with a class who suffers from low self esteem or motivation is one I shared at a CPD session that apparently had a huge impact on teachers and their classes. It was a PowerPoint presentation that contained specific positive comments about each member of the class.

For example, each slide could contain phrases such as those written in Table 8.1. Each slide has a positive comment about every student in the class with some kind of picture on it and with music playing across all slides. The presentation plays continuously (put it on continuous loop) during the time the class enter the classroom and this helps to create a positive and personalised atmosphere to the start of the lesson. The students feel that their efforts have been acknowledged in a public way and you have been able to start the lesson without making a negative comment which can be a problem with 'tricky' classes. It helps to create the right environment for learning by starting the lesson with a positive atmosphere.

Obviously, you don't want to overuse this strategy so once every two weeks will ensure novelty value and once the presentation is set up, it requires little editing from you each time.

Table 8.1 Creating a positive classroom environment

Hello Adam!	Brilliant work again today, please!
Morning Rosie!	Excellent homework!
Hello Luke!	Great teamwork last lesson.
Morning Freya!	Continue with brilliant contributions to class discussions.
Hello Will!	Keep up the challenge level today.
Morning Josh!	Fantastic focus yesterday. Keep it going!

Classroom assistants

Working with learning support assistants (LTA) in an English classroom can prove to be problematic due to lack of time to meet up and discuss the various techniques and strategies to use with specific students. Inevitably, English teachers have to rely on the high quality of the learning support assistants in order to help specific students and create the right learning environment for them.

However, a 'Working with additional adults' document such as the one in Table 8.2 might help you to overcome the time difficulty that you might have when working with learning support assistants.

This document can be quickly completed by you before each lesson and either emailed to the LTA in advance or handed to him/her as they enter the lesson. It also encourages the LTA to give you feedback about the progress of the students they have been working with which allows you to include that information in future planning.

Table 8.2 Working with additional adults

Lesson:	Date:	Time:

Learning activities: *(What are the pupils going to do?)*

Names of pupils: *(Identify individuals with specific learning needs)*

Subject/Area of learning and learning objectives: *(What are the pupils going to learn, develop, have practice with, be introduced to?)*

Resources used: *(Identify any specific resources)*

Key vocabulary/Key questions: *(Identify open-ended questions)*

Evaluation of the pupils' learning: *(TA to complete and share with the trainee)*

The 'Working with additional adults' document is one I created for trainee teachers to use in their classrooms, as working with LTAs is a new experience for many of them. However, this document has been adopted by many schools as it encapsulates good practice but within a short and concise document.

Outside learning

Taking students outside the classroom in schools is sometimes encouraged or discouraged depending on the culture of your school.

Theatre trips and visits to museums and places such as the Globe Theatre are obviously key activities that help to engage students with literature and make it come 'alive' for them as well as providing them with experiences that they might not have in their home life.

One outdoor activity that can be used within the playground is creating tension graphs of the plot development. First, in the classroom, discuss the tense moments of a novel, for example in *Lord of the Flies*, so that the students have an idea about what creates tension. Then go outside to the playground or a field and ask some students to create the vertical and horizontal axis of the tension graph and hold up cards that say Chapter 1, Chapter 5, Chapter 8 along the horizontal axis. Other students form the vertical axis and hold up cards with terms such as 'Low', 'Medium', 'High' etc. The rest of the students then place themselves at various points on the tension graph to represent specific moments in the novel. For example, Piggy's death; Simon's death etc. The whole space of the playground can be used to create this tension graph and in an ideal world, you would be able to run upstairs and take an aerial photo of the tension graph to show the visual impact of it. This tension graph can then be altered with the students and instructions from you depending on perspective: Is it the reader's perspective? Ralph's perspective? Piggy's perspective?

Once you have returned to the classroom, these photos can be shared with the students for class discussion or printed out to put in their books. The students then annotate the photos, inserting quotations to help support the judgements that were made within the tension graph.

Another one is called 'Four corners' and this can be used in a big space such as a drama hall or outside. Assign each corner a judgement, for example:

1) I strongly agree that capital punishment should be reinstated in this country.

2) I agree that capital punishment should be reinstated in this country.

3) I disagree that capital punishment should be reinstated in this country.

4) I strongly disagree that capital punishment should be reinstated in this country.

Ask the students to stand in whichever corner best matches their opinion. Then ask randomly selected students to explain their views about why they stood in the corner they did. Hear from just a few students and then play devil's advocate and say something such as, 'What would you do if I said, if capital punishment was reinstated then the executioner would be the victim. The victim of the serious crime would have to be the executioner. There would be no choice.'

Ask the students if that changes their mind for any reason and ask them to swap corners and choose whichever corner best matches their opinion. Again, ask some students to tell you why they swapped etc. You can then develop this further by asking more 'what if?' questions to help develop students' views from surface to deeper learning.

Another alternative to tension graphs and four corners is a continuum line. Again, in a big space, ask students to place themselves on a continuum line that represents opposing views from one end to the other. For example, at one end, their school should have a school uniform whereas at the other end the view is that their school should absolutely not have a school uniform. Ask a few students to justify their views about their position on the continuum line and then ask whether anyone has been persuaded to change their view. Again, ask some 'what if?' questions such as, 'What if the non-uniform clothes had to be yellow and you could only wear flip-flops?' Again, ask the students if that would change their minds and allow them to change their positions on the continuum line and ask them to share the reasons for their decision making. This type of activity can be extended by asking further 'what if' questions and encourage others students to join them at various points along the continuum line.

However, the key to making a success of the types of activities outlined is pace. Keeping the discussions brief and only hearing feedback from a few students is essential to ensuring that these type of activities are successful when not conducted within the confines of a traditional classroom. Again, taking photographs of the graphs, continuum lines and four corners allows you to develop further discussion about reasons and purposes for the changes and decisions made once you have returned to the classroom. These photographs can then be printed out for the students and annotated with additional information in order to ensure that the students have made connections between ideas and developed new learning from the activities.

Summary

The reality is that many teachers do not have the opportunity to only teach in one classroom and create their own wall displays and identity within the classroom anymore. Therefore, I have tried to include mainly activities to help create a positive learning physical and emotional environment that are transferable to any classroom.

For example, the role on the wall and poster activities with Post-it notes can easily be conducted within any classroom. The use of the voting pads may require some set up time but the use of the QR codes doesn't so they can easily be used in any classroom as can mini-whiteboards which provide the same sort of feedback about learning.

Another method to create a positive emotional learning environment is to establish rules of behaviour when learning is taking place. For example:

- Only one student talks at a time in group discussion.
- Everyone has the right to voice their opinion.
- Everyone stops talking at a given signal from the teacher '3, 2, 1' or hand up from the teacher.
- Everyone has the right to be listened to in group or class discussion.
- Any opinions must be discussed in an objective and not personal manner.

However, it can be difficult to display these in a classroom to use for future reference if you teach in a number of classrooms within a week. One solution is to create icons or abbreviations for the agreed behaviour points and display them as a small square in the corner of each of your presentation slides as a constant reminder about expectations for behaviour. You can just point to it at a particular moment in the lesson as a non-verbal reminder when students are not behaving correctly. Alternatively you can print them out on paper which you keep on your desk. An example is shown in Figure 8.1.

Figure 8.1 Setting behaviour expectations

However, it goes without saying that you as the teacher are the key factor in creating the right environment for learning for your students. Humour, patience, consistency and knowledge are the essential characteristics needed for any teacher to create the right environment but as outstanding teachers you already know that.

Reference

Berger, R. (2003) *An Ethic of Excellence*, Portsmouth: Heinemann.

CHAPTER 9

Putting it all together

This book has covered a range of teaching methods to ascertain progress in learning and this chapter is going to put some of these strategies into the context of two lessons. One from the poem 'Quickdraw' by Carol Ann Duffy aimed at Key Stage 4 students and one about persuasive language aimed at Key Stage 3 students.

Obviously you know the context and ability of your students so these lessons in their entirety may not completely fit your aims. However, the purpose of including these lessons is to demonstrate to you how incorporating the bell work, starter activity, learning outcomes, questioning and AfL strategies to gain information about student learning, and plenary activities can all be linked together when teaching 'stand alone' English lessons. Obviously, many lessons 'roll-on' from one to the other and may develop skills and knowledge over a period of three or four lessons but for the purpose of inclusion in this book, the two lessons are individual lessons where the learning is assessed at the start and the end of the lesson and opportunities are created to gain information about what the students know and do not know at various stages of the lesson.

There may be too many activities to include in one lesson as some schools have lessons that are 100 minutes and some that are 50 minutes. For that reason, I have purposefully avoided including timings in the lesson. However, the key aim of this lesson plan is to demonstrate the following:

- Progress of learning is checked at various points from all students.

- There are opportunities to address misconceptions.

- Students are encouraged to learn ideas independently.

- Range of teaching methods are used in the lesson and the inclusion of the music track at the start of the lesson without explanation helps to encourage curiosity from the students.

- Amount of new knowledge learned by the end of the lesson is ascertained by the use of the activities quiz, Exit Ticket and plenary.

Key Stage 4 lesson plan

Table 9.1 Lesson plan using 'Quickdraw' by Carol Ann Duffy

'Quickdraw' by Carol Ann Duffy	Commentary
Objective: To understand the meaning and poetic techniques of 'Quickdraw' by Carol Ann Duffy. *National Curriculum KS4 – Reading* • Identifying and interpreting themes, ideas and information • Seeking evidence in the text to support a point of view • Analysing a writer's choice of language	The objective is taken from the National Curriculum taught from September 2015.
Outcomes: • **Identify** the language features in the poem to create an effect for the reader. • **Interpret** the impact of the language in conveying the meaning of the poem to the reader.	The verbs for the outcomes are taken from Bloom's Taxonomy and Webb's DOK levels. Students can write these outcomes down in their exercise books in the style of the continuum line as outlined in the starter activity or they can write down the 'Big Question' for the lesson.
Big question: How do the metaphors in the poem 'Quickdraw' help to create a picture of a fractured relationship?	
Bell work: (From *The Little Book of Thunks* by Ian Gilbert (2007.) • If you could take a pill that meant you would never fail, would you? • Would you play the lottery if there was more chance of winning but also of losing everything?	These 'thunks' are displayed on the board as the students enter the room. Give students a Post-it note to write down their initial thoughts to these questions. Using bell work in this way indicates to the students that learning and thinking starts as soon as they enter your classroom. Choose two students to hear ideas from very briefly. Make it clear that are no are right ideas.
Starter: Continuum line asking students to indicate their level of confidence in being able to identify ideas in a poem independently and write about their meaning. ◄─────────────────────► Don't Feel Feel feel quite confident confident confident Also play Katie Perry's 'Firework' in the background while students are completing this task and tell them that you will come back to the reason for this later in the lesson.	Students can indicate their level of confidence on mini-whiteboards, QR codes or using voting pads against this continuum line. You could show a few sentences of writing that demonstrate the skills of being able to identify ideas in this poem so the students have a model to use to gauge their feelings of confidence against.

Continued

Table 9.1 Continued

'Quickdraw' by Carol Ann Duffy	Commentary
This continuum line provides you with feedback about how many students feel confident about analysing a poem themselves and how many do not. This then allows you to work out which students need which questions about the poem which I discussed in Chapter 5.	You need to ask at least three students in the class who represent the different groups that exist in your class, e.g. ability, Special Educational Needs (SEN), Free School Meals (FSM) • Why have you placed yourself at that point on the continuum line? • What do you think you need to do in order to achieve the learning outcome of the lesson? • What do you think I need to do in order to help you achieve the skill of being able to identify ideas in a poem and write about their meaning?
Starter: Watch a clip of *High Noon* (1952) where the sheriff walks into town to have a gun battle with some baddies. Display a collage of pictures about the Wild West including ones of a silver bullet and Last Chance saloon.	Think Pair Share – ask students individually to think about the words and ideas that they would associate with the video clip and also the pictures on the board. Then ask them briefly to discuss with each other. Ask any students to contribute and give some ideas as no need for hands-up as they have had time to discuss with each other.
Main: Give out the poem 'Quickdraw' by Carol Ann Duffy with some key words missing and ask the students to complete the missing words by referring to words from a word bank at the bottom of the page. Word bank may contain words such as 'text, belt, quickdraw, blast, silver bullet, deadly'. Make sure that the word bank contains more words than missing words. Return to learning outcome about how meaning of poem is conveyed through language and point out that they made many of those judgements about the poem with little support from you.	1) Students to independently complete cloze activity. 2) Students to talk in pairs and agree a common version. 3) Show students Duffy's version and then a class discussion about why they made the decisions they did. What clues did they use to choose the words they did? Can ask any student to contribute to this discussion as had opportunities to discuss in pairs. 4) What do they think this poem is about? 5) Refer back to the first slide for the starter with the images of the Wild West on it and ask them to highlight all the words they think are connected with the Wild West. 6) Then show the students a completed highlighted version identifying words connected with Wild West terms so they can check their answers.

'Quickdraw' by Carol Ann Duffy	Commentary
Main: Display a slide with three definitions of a metaphor on it: 1) A metaphor is a term that describes something as being like something else. 2) A metaphor is a term that describes something in a manner that cannot be real. 3) A metaphor is a term that describes things that are opposite to each other.	Ask the students using either mini-whiteboards, voting pads, QR codes or any other AfL strategy to indicate which meaning they think is right. This will then tell you who knows the correct meaning of a metaphor and depending on your knowledge of your class you might need to have some examples of metaphors to help reinforce what a metaphor looks like. Asking for feedback in this way from every student will help you to address misconceptions.
Main: Ask students to highlight in their copy of the poem all the metaphors they can find.	Once students have completed the highlighting activity then show them a copy of the poem with the metaphors highlighted. How many of them have the same version as you? Again, this allows you to find out where the misconceptions are and who to target in the next section.
Main: Display a slide with the meaning of an extended metaphor. • An extended metaphor is a poetic technique that continues over multiple lines and is sometimes extended throughout an entire poem. Once the term extended metaphor has been explored, introduce the term 'conceit'. • A technique used in a poem that compares a situation in an exaggerated way to something else is called a 'conceit' and in this case it is a 'shoot-out' in the poem 'Quickdraw'.	You can link examples of an extended metaphor to previous learning or ask the students to think about anything they have heard or read about today which could be an extended metaphor. Some students may pick up the old western style gunfight extended metaphor in the poem 'Quickdraw' but others may remember about Katie Perry's 'Firework' being played. Then discuss why the song 'Firework' is an extended metaphor and you may wish to display the lyrics. This is an example of clear differentiation as students will respond to the question about the extended metaphor differently either from the poem or via the song lyrics but neither answer is wrong.
Main: Ask students to highlight/underline all the words that are connected with a 'shoot-out'. Return to the Big Question for the lesson: How do the metaphors in this poem help to create a picture of a fractured relationship?	Students need to write down the definition of conceit and how it is used in the poem 'Quickdraw'. Short pair discussion about the Big Question and then ask a few students (without hands-up) for their answers to the Big Question at this point of the lesson.

Continued

Table 9.1 Continued

'Quickdraw' by Carol Ann Duffy	Commentary

Main:

Refer back to the learning outcomes as the questions for the poem are helping them to be able to identify and interpret more independently which is why they are doing this activity.

- Independently **identify** the language features used in the poem to create an effect for the reader.
- Independently **interpret** the impact of the language in conveying the meaning of the poem to the reader.

Give the students a copy of the poem with the questions inserted or display it on the board. The questions are in Chapter 5 (see page 57). At this stage, you can direct how many of the questions you want the students to answer.

Once the students have completed the question activity then a typical teaching strategy is to go through each question and ask for feedback from various individuals and encourage a class discussion. I would argue that an alternative strategy would be to show the students the answers to the questions to fit with the learning outcomes; this lesson is encouraging the students to independently identify and interpret ideas within a poem. Yes, there has been scaffolding by the use of the questions to support differentiation but haven't the students engaged with the learning by answering the questions and creating their own answers? Does there need to be a class discussion to validate their answers?

I would suggest that an alternative to a class discussion would be to display the answers to the questions that the students have been engaging with and ask them to ensure that they have not misunderstood any of the ideas. There is an opportunity to address any misconceptions while the students are checking their version and yours although it is important to stress that there is not a typical right answer.

Plenary:

Quick quiz to check learning of terms and ideas within the poem to ascertain that the ability to identify and interpret ideas in this poem has been learned.

1) Is this line a simile or a metaphor? 'I wear the two, the mobile and the landline phones, like guns, slung from the pockets on my hips'.
2) Is this line a simile or a metaphor? 'Your voice a pellet in my ear'.
3) Explain in five words how 'high noon, calamity and Last Chance saloon' all link to the conceit of the poem.
4) Explain in five words how a 'silver bullet' is relevant to the conceit of the poem.
5) Explain in eight words the meaning of the title 'Quickdraw'.

By asking students to complete the answers to this quiz in a specific number of words it is possible to quickly review their answers either on a mini-whiteboard or through a voting pad. If reading all the answers on mini-whiteboards is too difficult due to the number of students within the room then taking a photo of the class with their answers on an iPad will give you the opportunity to assess the knowledge in the room before the end of the lesson.

This quiz is identifying who knows where some of the language features are and whether the conceit of a gun fight or Wild West have been learned by all.

You could ask this quiz earlier in the lesson after the cloze activity once the students have read and engaged with the poem and see how many of them can answer the questions. Doing the quiz twice would clearly ascertain progress of learning but equally doing it as part of the plenary demonstrates the number of students who can accurately identify the language features in the poem by the end of the lesson which links with the learning outcomes.

'Quickdraw' by Carol Ann Duffy	Commentary
Exit Ticket – can differentiate the Exit Ticket and give the students a choice to answer: In order to answer today's Big Question 'How do the metaphors in the poem help to create a picture of a fractured relationship in the poem?', you need to do one of the following: • Write down three sentences that describe the state of the relationship in the poem 'Quickdraw'. Give an example of one metaphor to support your sentences. • What is the conceit that runs throughout this poem? Provide one example of a metaphor that supports this conceit. Explain in three sentences what the conceit tells about the state of the relationship.	In order to answer the Big Question 'How do the metaphors in the poem help to create a picture of a fractured relationship in the poem?', students need to be able to demonstrate to you that they can answer the Big Question which will mean that they can meet the learning outcomes. Unlike asking for a paragraph of writing, an Exit Ticket gives clear instructions about the amount of writing that should be included. The Exit Ticket can be given out to students to complete and these can then be collated within the student portfolio as discussed in Chapter 6.

Plenary:

A final plenary activity could be to repeat the continuum line activity to ascertain whether any of the students have gained in confidence about their ability to independently identify ideas in a poem.

However, certain students (who represent specific groups e.g. ability; SEN; FSM) should be asked the questions after they have placed themselves on the continuum line:

• What did you do today to help you gain in confidence about being able to identify ideas in a poem?
• What poetic features do you think you will be able to recognise by yourself in other poems?
• What did I do today to help you gain in confidence and knowledge about recognising poetic features in poems?

In accordance with current research about strategies that help students to retain information, the terminology of an extended metaphor and a conceit would be checked at the start of the next lesson and then on a regular monthly basis. It could be included as a quiz at the start of a lesson or just one of a list of multiple choice questions that are presented to the students at regular intervals. A recent document from an organisation called Deans for Impact summarises research from cognitive science about how students learn. The document is called Science for Learning www.deansforimpact.org/the_science_of_learning.html.

One of the teaching methods that the document suggests is successful is called interleaving, where central ideas are intertwined with other concepts and returned to at various points. The document suggests that there is no need to teach a scheme of work purely about metaphors and extended metaphors as it would be more beneficial to return to these poetic terms regularly within the context of other topics. The same would apply to grammar. Teaching students about grammar in isolation may not be as useful as teaching grammar terminology and its uses within other schemes of work and revisiting at various intervals.

Putting it all together

This type of approach might help with the learning of quotations for the closed book exam which is part of the new specifications being taught from September 2015. This research is suggesting that interleaving but also story-telling and mnemonics are successful teaching strategies for helping students to recall information that they have to learn for an exam.

Key Stage 3 lesson plan

I have also written a lesson plan that is about teaching or building on students' knowledge about persuasive language. I have not assigned a specific year to the lesson plan but have used the National Curriculum criteria for KS3 as a purpose for the lesson.

I have not given all the resource material that you might need for this lesson as again it will depend on the context of your class and what you think is appropriate. However, I hope it encapsulates many of the strategies that I have discussed in the book and the commentary helps to explain the purpose of the strategies.

Table 9.2 Teaching persuasive techniques

National Curriculum – KS3
<ul><li>Writing for a wide range of purposes and audiences</li><li>Writing in a range of non-narrative texts</li><li>Drawing on knowledge of rhetorical devices to enhance the impact of their writing</li></ul>

Persuasive writing	Commentary
Objective: To be able to use persuasive devices in speech and writing to effectively persuade an audience.	This objective is taken from the Programmes of Study for KS3 National Curriculum 2013.
Outcomes: <ul><li>**Define** features of persuasive language in spoken and written language.</li><li>**Assess** the impact of persuasive language on an audience.</li><li>**Create** a piece of writing using persuasive language about a product aimed at a specific audience.</li></ul>	The verbs for the outcomes are taken from Bloom's Taxonomy and Webb's DOK levels. Students can write these outcomes down in their exercise books or they can write down the 'Big Question' for the lesson.

Big Question: What impact can persuasive language have on an audience when it is done well?

Bell work:

A PowerPoint slide taken from www. presentationmagazine.com/powerpoint-jigsaw-puzzle-1942.htm where an image of Martin Luther King is revealed.

No need to look at the speeches but just linking the bell work activity to the idea that the lesson is going to be about persuasive language. Can introduce the learning outcomes at this stage of the lesson or not.

Students to take turns to press the button to reveal the picture underneath or you as the teacher control the animations of the pieces of the puzzle.
- What do they know about Martin Luther King? What did he represent? When he did live? Why did he die? What was he famous for?
- Leading them to the idea of 'I have a Dream' speech as one of the most persuasive speeches in modern time. Could do the same with a picture of Henry V and link it to the St Crispin's Day speech if appropriate for class.

Starter:

Watch just over the first two minutes of the video clip about the introduction of the Magic Wand remote on *Dragons' Den* when the product is introduced and stop before the Dragons start to ask questions. www.youtube.com/watch?v=hp5gTE9ZScw Do not teach any of the features of persuasive language; just ask for students to identify as many as they can with no input from you. You could organise the persuasive features on an Entrance Ticket which the students tick as they note which ones are used in the video clip.

Students to tick off as many persuasive techniques that they can recognise from the clip. Depending on the context of your class, you may ask them to watch and listen and write down as many features as they can find without a list of terms at all.
Might have to watch it a couple of times.
- rhetorical questions
- present negative and positive features of the product
- inclusive pronouns
- hyperbole and superlatives
- repetition
- emotive language
- rule of three
- anecdotes

Students to show to you on mini-whiteboards or voting pads which persuasive strategies they think were present in the video clip. Need to keep a note of which students said hyperbole, rule of three and emotive language as they are the ones that demonstrate a high level of understanding of persuasive language.

Do make the link that many persuasive teaching strategies in spoken language are relevant in writing too.

Generate a class discussion by asking individuals in the class if they thought the video clip was successful in demonstrating persuasive language. Pose that as the key question and then Pounce and Bounce the ideas around so that at least four or five students have given their opinion, using the technique as discussed in Chapter 5. Try to offer no opinion of your own at this stage or acknowledge that it was good or bad.

By not asking the class for features of persuasive language as a brainstorm at the start of the lesson or giving them feedback about the clip, it is easier to establish what they know.

Continued

Table 9.2 Continued

National Curriculum – KS3

Main:

Introduce the concepts of hyperbole, emotive language and rule of three to the class from a text that you think is appropriate for them.

You could use extracts from 'I have a Dream' speech by Martin Luther King to link with the bell work activity.

This part of the lesson is now only focused on teaching the missing knowledge in the class. Students that you recognise as having the knowledge based on the feedback from the previous activity can be the ones that you question at the start of the introduction to each persuasive language feature.

For example, 'Rosie, can you identify for me an example of the use of rule of three in Martin Luther King's speech and why is it being used?' This is demonstrating how your teaching is being affected by the amount of knowledge that students have as you are reacting to their feedback.

Try to avoid teaching about all the persuasive features in any speech that you choose – try and just focus on the ones that the students didn't know based on the *Dragon's Den* clip.

Return to the Big Question:

What impact can persuasive language have on an audience when it is done well?

Before moving on to the next activity, ask a few students from specific groups in your class, e.g. SEN, FSM, high or low ability to answer this Big Question. This checks whether the students have been able to understand the impact of the persuasive strategies that you have just taught them.

Do not tell the students that they are about to watch a 'poor' version of another example of persuasive language.

Main:

Watch a poor example of a *Dragon's Den* presentation about an egg timer www.youtube.com/watch?v=LBiUOw7rNps

However, do not tell the students that this is a poor version but ask them to identify how many persuasive techniques there are in this presentation.

Then ask them to pair up to discuss their ideas and ask any group for a contribution. How many can they find? What are the problems?

Giving the students a 'poor' version at this point of the lesson helps to determine whether they can actually identify features of persuasive language.

- Would they be expecting you to give them another good example?
- What does it tell you about their depth of learning as you are asking them to transfer their knowledge into another context, e.g. a poor example of persuasive language.

Main:

Now, the students need to create success criteria for successful persuasive language. Do they agree that similar features are needed for spoken or written persuasive language?

Asking the students to create success criteria for persuasive language demonstrates that they have learned the information.

Tell students that they are going to have to 'sell' a product so what success criteria are they going to use in their persuasive language? Ask them to get into pairs to brainstorm a few ideas that they think should be in their language for 'pitch' about a product.

Putting the task into a real context such as a 'sales pitch' helps to give it a relevance to them at this stage. Try to avoid giving any information about the 'sales' pitch and product as again this will add to curiosity.

Ask the pairs to share ideas and then rank the best ones so that they create the joint top four features of persuasive language that should be in their writing.

Asking students to pair and share but then rank their joint ideas helps to increase accountability and also ensures that their learning goes from surface to deeper learning as to rank ideas they are using some kind of selection criteria which again demonstrates learning.

Hear from each group one of their ideas to create an agreed set of class success criteria for successful persuasive language.

Creating class success criteria means that you can pitch it at the right level for your class.

Main:

Next, show to the class a bag that contains a range of items that they are going to use to deliver an 'elevator' pitch to you and other classmates as potential customers.

The bag of products needs to contain everyday items such as a teaspoons, a mug, sellotape, a candle and a pencil. Try and ensure that there is a different item for each pair. Each pair then draws out their item from the bag.

You may wish to share a model of a 30 second elevator pitch to the class on an everyday product that you might have in your class. Alternatively, you may wish to model the task that follows about a product so they understand about how creative they need to be about the product's uses.

An elevator pitch is a short speech that is either 30 seconds or 60 seconds long – the length of time that it takes a lift to go from the ground floor to the top floor of a tall building. Taken from the advertising world where clients would tell advertisers that they had the length of the 'elevator ride' to pitch them their ideas.

You could give the class a structure for this task as follows:
- four minutes to brainstorm all the qualities of their product;
- four minutes to brainstorm all the creative uses of their product;
- three minutes to decide the types of persuasive language they are going to use in their writing.

By structuring the preparation of the task in this way, you are ensuring that the following is taking place:
- students complete each stage of the task;
- task appears broken down so it seems accessible – not open ended;
- students have time to verbalise their thoughts and ideas with each other so have support in planning;
- students have been encouraged to think about each part of the task which will help them to complete it successfully.

Give a period of time for the writing of the elevator pitch that you think is appropriate, but make sure they understand the audience is their class mates.

Continued

Putting it all together

Table 9.2 Continued

National Curriculum – KS3	
Plenary: Using the success criteria, students assess each other's elevator speeches – can either assess each other's writing or they can deliver the speech to the class or each other verbally.	Model to the students an example of a successful peer assessment so that they understand your expectations. The comments should only be related to the success criteria and you may wish to introduce the 'what went well' or 'even better if' or 'two stars and a wish' structure to help the students organise their peer assessment comments.
Return to the Big Question: What impact can persuasive language have on an audience when it is done well? Ask the students to write in their books, on a whiteboard, or on an Exit Ticket their answer to the Big Question. How did successful persuasive language make them feel? What did it make them want to do? They need to give some specific examples from the lesson of where they heard or read successful persuasive language.	The students have now been the audience of language and have seen a range of good or bad examples of persuasive language so should be able to answer this Big Question successfully. However, if you asked them to write an answer at the start of the lesson then it wouldn't have contained specific references to language and ideas as it does now at the end of the lesson.

I have planned this as one lesson but I realise that depending on the length of lessons in your school there is probably enough material to generate a couple of lessons.

However, the purpose of this lesson plan was to demonstrate that:

- 'testing' pupils' knowledge at the start of the lesson, e.g. watching the video clip with little input from you as the teacher, helps you to gain feedback about what knowledge the students have;

- opportunities are created in the lesson to teach to the 'gaps' in the students' knowledge rather than just teaching all the strategies that can exist in persuasive language;

- success criteria can be used explicitly to help with the quality of peer assessment;

- curiosity can be generated for students by the use of everyday items;

- structuring the steps to a task is important so it is not too open ended and appears unobtainable;

- giving students time to verbally plan their ideas together is helpful;

- the Big Question can be answered at the end of the lesson in a meaningful way;

- giving a context to the learning of the lesson, e.g. an elevator pitch, is essential.

Summary

Planning a lesson should always focus on the *learning* that the students need to achieve by the end of the lesson rather than what they should have *done* by the end of the lesson.

The purpose of the learning should be taken from the National Curriculum or Assessment Objectives from exam specifications.

Key questions you should ask yourself when planning lessons are:

- What are the students going to know by the end of the lesson that they didn't know at the start?

- How are you going to check that 'starting point' in their knowledge? What AfL strategies are you going to use?

- How are you going to check their learning by the end of the lesson? What AfL strategies are you going to use?

- How are you going to check progress against the learning outcomes or ability to answer the Big Question throughout the lesson? What AfL strategies are you going to use?

- How are you going to ensure that all students are accountable for their contribution to tasks?

- How are you going to make it clear what success looks like for the task?

- How are you going to encourage curiosity about the topic?

- How are you going to ensure that all students engage with new concepts at least a few times in a lesson, e.g. new terminology. Are there opportunities for the students to read it, write it and speak it at least once in a lesson?

- How are you going to link the lesson's learning to previous learning so the new learning doesn't look too difficult?

- How are you going to ensure that there is a pace to the lesson and the right combination of student led or teacher led activities?

- How are you going to ensure that you have included high order and low order questions and engaged a range of students in answering the questions?

- How are you going to check that the learning outcomes are reached by the end of the lesson?

By answering these questions, you will ensure that you are well on the way to planning high quality lessons that have learning at the centre of them.

Reference

Gilbert, I. (2007) *The Little Book of Thunks: 260 Questions to Make Your Brain Go Ouch!* Carmarthen: Crown House Publishing.

Conclusion

The aim of this book is to provide you with a range of resources and strategies that can be used in your teaching practice on a daily basis. There is no 'quick fix' and you might find that some of the strategies might not work first time. However, that does not mean that you should not continue and persevere if you feel that you and your students will benefit from taking a different approach to the one that you are currently using. Remember, it can also take time to overcome a certain mindset of expectations by the students about how they learn in your classroom.

For example, in Chapter 5, you may wish to stop validating each student's answer during a question and answer session. Therefore, before you adopt this strategy you may need to explain that your non-verbal signal of a nod of the head and a smile indicates that you are happy with their comment. This will be a slight change for the students but one they will quickly become accustomed to and it will result in greater student engagement in discussions.

A few key questions to ask yourself when planning and teaching lessons are as follows. These underpin many of the strategies that are used in this book.

- What is the learning going to be in this lesson? Not the 'doing', but the 'learning'?
- What do the students know at the end of the lesson that they didn't know at the start of the lesson? How do I know?
- Are the students working more or less hard in this lesson than I am?
- Is every student contributing to the learning? How can I tell?
- What is the brilliant outcome for this lesson or number of lessons? What does the 'best it can be' look like for this topic or skill?

As English teachers, we know the importance of our subject and the impact it can have on our students' lives. I hope that this book, in a small way, might make your life easier as it will provide you with some more ideas to include in your daily teaching strategies.

Index

Note: Page numbers followed by 'f' refer to figures and followed by 't' refer to tables.

3-2-1 40

'Ask Me What I Have Learned Today?' 46
assessable verbs 80, 80f, 82
assessment 62–75; colour coded learning outcomes 66–8, 69; encouraging reflection time 70–2; Entrance and Exit tickets 68–9, 68t; formative 62; key questions 63; for learning 62; of learning 63; as learning 63; learning outcomes and success criteria 64–9; marking as a form of 72–3; photographs of students work 74, 75; quality of interactions with students 69–70; student led success criteria 65–6; summative 63; without levels 73–5
assessment activity, main 26–35; lesson plans 102–4t, 108–9t; poetry 30–4; reading 28–30; writing 26–7, 27t
Assessment for Learning (AfL) strategies 16
autism 84

Beere, Jackie 70
behaviour rules 98, 98f
bell work 8–11; lesson plans 101t, 107t
Berger, Ron 74–5, 89
Big Question 15; lesson plans 101t, 106t, 108t, 110t; revisiting 39–40
Blackburn, Barbara 26
blogs 47
Bloom Buster 78–9

Bloom's Taxonomy 12, 54, 56, 78–80
brilliant learning outcomes 13–14, 24–5, 38–9
Brown, George 60
Burns, Mark 60
Buzan, Tony 85
Buzz Word Bingo 18

challenge/extension task 84
Circle of Ideas 27
classroom assistants 86–7, 87t, 94–6, 95t
classroom environment 89–99; classroom assistants 94–6, 95t; displays 89–90; group work 91–2; outside learning 96–7; positive learning environment 93–4, 94t; rules of behaviour 98, 98f; seating plans 93; student contribution in lessons 90–1
Classroom Instruction 26
colour coded learning outcomes 13, 66–8, 69
coloured pens 71, 72
coloured trays for exercise books 37–8
Conscience Alley 29
continuum lines: brilliant learning outcomes 14, 14f, 38–9; to check prior knowledge 17–18, 17f; lesson plans 101–2t; outside learning 97

de Bono, Edward 28
Deans for Impact 4, 75, 105
Depth of Knowledge (DOK) 54–6, 55t

differentiation 76–88; challenge/extension task 84; by learning outcomes 82–3; by questioning 78–9; with students with specific learning needs 84–6; support notes 86; by task 80–1; teaching assistants 86–7, 87t; visual images 86
dingbats 11, 11f
DIRT (Dedicated, Improvement, Reflection Time) 70–2
displays, classroom 89–90
Dweck, Dr Carol 4–5
dyslexia 85–6
dyspraxia 85

end of lesson 37–48; big question 39–40; home learning 45–7; learning outcomes 37–8; lesson plans 104–5t, 110t; plenary activities 40–3; reflection 43–5
English as an Additional Language 86
Entrance Tickets 11, 68, 68t
An Ethic of Excellence 74–5, 89
excellence, aiming for 74–5
Exit Tickets 40–1, 68, 68t, 69, 74; lesson plans 105t, 110t

F.E.A.R. 50–1
feedback, four levels of 69–70
folders, A4 67–8, 69, 74, 75
Four Corners 96–7
fragmenting a poem 32–3

Gershon, Mike 78
Gilbert, Ian 9
Ginnis, Paul 12, 13, 37, 49, 80, 80f, 82
GoogleDocs 47
Griffith, Andy 60
group work 91–2
growth mindsets 4–5
'guess the learning objective' jigsaw 9–10, 10f

Hattie, John 17f, 69, 70
home learning 45–7

IDEA 60
'If (name of character) was an object' 20
interleaving 105–6

jigsaw, 'guess the learning objective' 9–10, 10f

Key Stage 3 lesson plan 106–10
Key Stage 4 lesson plan 101–6
knowledge, checking prior 15–18; continuum lines 17–18, 17f; for differentiation 77; KWL grid 18, 18t; quizzes 15–17
knowledge, depth of 54–6, 55t
KWL grid: to check prior learning 18, 18t; for student reflection 43–4

learning in the main 23–36; assessment activity 26–35; class level of engagement 23–4; lesson plans 102–4t, 108–9t; poetry 30–4; reading 28–30; sequencing the learning 24–6; writing 26–7, 27t
learning journey: of students 4–5; of teachers 5–6
learning outcomes: brilliant 13–14, 24–5, 38–9; colour coded 13, 66–8, 69; differentiation by 82–3; as distinct from learning objectives 12; lesson plans 101t, 106t; at plenary stage 37–8; as questions 49–51; at start of lesson 12–14; students choosing own 13; and success criteria 64–9; verbs and 12–13, 37, 66–7
Learning Partners seating plan 93
'Learning Principles & Planning Prompts' 12, 13, 80
lesson plans: key aims 100; Key Stage 3 106–10; Key Stage 4 101–6
levels of feedback 69–70
'lighthouse' scanning 23–4
Lucky Dip 20

main assessment activity 26–35; lesson plans 102–4t, 108–9t; poetry 30–4; reading 28–30; writing 26–7, 27t
marking: colour-coded trays for 37–8; as a form of assessment 72–3
McGill, Ross 45, 52
mind mapping 85
Mindset: How You Can Fulfill Your Potential 5

mini-whiteboards 15, 16, 41, 42, 47
motivating students 6–7

noise levels 23

observation of students: and colleagues 5–6; to 'read' a class and level of engagement 23–4
outside learning 96–7
outstanding lessons 2–3

parents involvement in homework 45, 46
peer assessment 25, 26, 44, 63, 65
The Perfect Ofsted Lesson 70
personalising learning 76
persuasive: techniques 25–6, 106–10t; writing 50–1
photographs: assessment 74, 75; Big Question 15; classroom displays 89; end of lesson 45, 47; generating student questions 59; learning in main 30; outside learning 97; starter activities 19, 21
Pictionary 20–1
pictures as a bell work activity 10, 10f
plans, essay 24–5
plenary activities 40–3; lesson plans 104t, 105t, 110t
poetry: fragmenting a poem 32–3; lesson plan 101–6; source of words 33–4, 34t; teaching 30–4; written questions 56–8, 57f
'Pose, Pause, Pounce, Bounce' (PPPB) 52–4
positive learning environment 93–4, 94t
Post-it notes: classroom displays 89; and differentiation by task 81; filing 74; group work 92; learning outcomes 13, 66, 67; reflection and targets 43–4
prior knowledge, checking 15–18; continuum lines 17–18, 17f; for differentiation 77; KWL grid 18, 18t; quizzes 15–17
progress charts 41–2, 41t
Progress Partners seating plan 93
props 7

Questioning in the Secondary School 60
questions 49–61; and answer sessions, teacher as funnel for 51–2; to ask when planning lessons 111; asking students 16, 58; Big Question 15, 39–40; Depth of Knowledge levels 54–6, 55t; differentiation by 78–9; learning outcomes as 49–51; 'Pose, Pause, Pounce, Bounce' 52–4; refusing to answer for 3 minutes 24; students generating own 58–60; written 56–8, 57f
'questions for the future' homework strategy 46–7
quick response (QR) codes 90, 91
'Quickdraw': lesson plan 101–5t; written questions 57f
quizzes: to check prior knowledge 15–17; end of lesson 42, 104t; home learning 46; lesson plans 104t; for preparation of closed book exams 16–17
quotes, learning: home learning 46; interleaving 106; quizzes 16–17; True/False cards 42; visual ways of learning 20–1

RAFT 26, 27t
random name generator 90
reading main assessment activity 28–30
reflection: encouraging time for 70–2; strategies 43–5
research on how students learn 105–6
Role on the Wall 29–30
Rowe, Mary Budd 52

scheme of work 4–5
The Science of Learning 4, 75, 105
seating plans 93
self-assessment: of learning outcomes 37–8; progress charts 41–2, 41t; success criteria for 65–6
sequencing the learning 24–6
sharing stories 6
Silent Debate 18–20
SIR 44–5, 71–2
Six Thinking Hats 28–9, 28t
source of words 33–4, 34t
specific learning needs, students with 84–6
start of lesson 8–22; bell work 8–11; Big Question 15; checking prior knowledge 15–18; examples 22; learning outcomes 12–14; starter activities 14–15, 18–21

Index

starter activities 14–15, 18–21; lesson plans 101–2t, 107t
student contribution in lessons 90–1
student led success criteria 65–6
student portfolios 74–5, 90
success criteria: and learning outcomes 64–9; student led 65–6
support notes 86

Take Away Homework 45
task, differentiation by 80–1
Teacher's Toolkit 12, 13
teaching assistants 86–7, 87t, 94–6, 95t
Teaching Backwards 60
tension graphs 96
Thinking Hats 28–9, 28t
'thunks' 9
Tic-Tac-Toe 34, 35t
topical links to events and issues 6
True/False cards 42–3
Twitter 47
'two stars and a wish' 44, 65

verbs: assessable 80, 80f, 82; differentiation in teaching use of 77; learning outcomes and 12–13, 37, 66–7
Visible Learning 69
visual images: bell work activities 9–10, 10f; for children with English as an Additional Language 86; for learning of quotes 20–1; for learning outcomes 83
voting pads 90–1
Vygotsky, Lev 2

'wait time' 52
Webb, Dr Norman 54
website, school 46
Working with Additional Adults 94–6, 95t
Wragg, Edward 60
writing: main assessment activity 26–7, 27t; persuasive 50–1
written questions 56–8, 57f

Zone of Proximal Development 2